Quips,
Quotes,
and
Quests

Quips, Quotes, and Quests

Vern McLellan

HARVEST HOUSE PUBLISHERS
Eugene, Oregon 97402

Except where otherwise indicated, all Scripture quotations in this book are taken from The Living Bible, Copyright 1971 by Tyndale House Publishers, Wheaton, Illinois. Used by permission.

QUIPS, QUOTES & QUESTS

Copyright ©1982 Harvest House Publishers
Eugene, Oregon 97402

Library of Congress Catalog Card Number 81-85544
ISBN 0-89081-310-8

Printed in the United States of America.

Quip:　　Mark Twain once made the following New Year's resolution: "I'm going to live within my income this year if I have to borrow money to do it."

Quote:　　"No, dear brothers, I am still not all I should be, but I am bringing all my energies to bear this one thing: Forgetting the past and looking forward to what lies ahead, I strain to reach the end of the race and receive the prize for which God is calling us up to heaven because of what Christ Jesus did for us" (Philippians 3: 13,14).

Quest:　　What the New Year brings to you will depend a great deal on what you are bringing to the New Year.

★

Quip:　　Some people remind us of French bread—one long loaf.

Quote:　　"For you well know that you ought to follow our example: you never saw us loafing; we never accepted food from anyone without buying it; we worked hard day and night for the money we needed to live on, in order that we would not be a burden to any of you" (2 Thessalonians 3: 7,8).

Quest:　　What the world needs is fewer bakers and more delivery boys.

Quip: Life for some people is to sow wild oats during the week and then go to church Sunday and pray for a crop failure.

Quote: "Don't be misled; remember that you can't ignore God and get away with it: a man will always reap just the kind of crop he sows!" (Galatians 6:7)

Quest: Let us endeavor to so live that when we come to die, even the undertaker will be sorry (Mark Twain).

★

Quip: If you must cry over spilt milk, condense it.

Quote: "For I admit my shameful deed—it haunts me day and night . . .Create in me a new, clean heart, O God, filled with clean thoughts and right desires . . .Restore to me again the joy of your salvation, and make me willing to obey you" (Psalm 51: 3, 10, 12).

Quest: Regret can be an appalling waste of energy—you can't build on it. So acknowledge your sin, accept God's forgiveness, and get on with living for His honor and glory.

Quip: A loose tongue often gets its owner into a tight place.

Quote: "Self-control means controlling the tongue! A quick retort can ruin everything" (Proverbs 13:3).

Quest: Usually the first screw that gets loose in a person's head is the one that controls the tongue.

★

Quip: The horn of plenty is the one the guy behind you has on his car (Crane).

Quote: "Now as for you, dear brothers who are waiting for the Lord's return, be patient, like a farmer who waits until the autumn for his precious harvest to ripen" (James 5:7).

Quest: Adopt the pace of nature: Her secret is patience.

Quip: An ulcer is what you get mountain-
climbing over molehills.

Quote: "Don't worry about anything; instead,
pray about everything; tell God your
needs and don't forget to thank him for
his answers" (Philippians 4:6).

Quest: There are two days you should not
worry about—yesterday and tomorrow.

★

Quip: Father, after checking his son's report
card: "There's one thing in your favor:
With these grades, you couldn't possibly
have been cheating."

Quote: "The Lord hates cheating and delights in
honesty" (Proverbs 11:1).

Quest: The first and worst of all frauds is to
cheat yourself.

Quip: He who will not economize may have to agonize.

Quote: "The wise man saves for the future, but the foolish man spends whatever he gets" (Proverbs 21: 20).

Quest: The secret of economy is to live as cheaply the first few days after payday as you did the last few days before.

★

Quip: Sign in window: The difficult we will do right away; the impossible may take a little longer.

Quote: "Jesus looked at them intently, then said, 'Without God, it is utterly impossible. But with God everything is possible'" (Mark 10:27).

Quest: You never test the resources of God until you attempt the impossible. The life motto of Missionary William Cary was, "Attempt great things for God; expect great things from God."

Quip: A hug is a roundabout way of
               expressing affection.

Quote: "Love each other with brotherly affec-
               tion and take delight in honoring each
               other" (Romans 12:10).

Quest: Respect is what we owe; love is what we
               give (Bailey).

                              ★

Quip: If you aim at nothing, you're sure to
               hit it.

Quote: "So I run straight to the goal with pur-
               pose in every step. I fight to win. I'm not
               just shadow-boxing or playing around"
               (1 Corinthians 9:26).

Quest: Aim for the top. There is plenty of room
               there. There are so few at the top that it
               is almost lonely (Insull).

Quip: You've got to do your own growing, no matter how tall your grandfather was.

Quote: "But grow in spiritual strength and become better acquainted with our Lord and Savior Jesus Christ. To him be all glory and spendid honor, both now and forevermore" (2 Peter 3:18).

Quest: Voyager upon life's sea: To yourself be true, and whate'er your lot may be, paddle your own canoe (Philpots).

★

Quip: If you must kill time, work it to death.

Quote: "Hard work means prosperity; only a fool idles away his time" (Proverbs 12:11).

Quest: One thing you can learn by watching the clock is that it passes the time by keeping its hands busy.

Quip: Too many people conduct their lives on
the cafeteria plan—self-service only.

Quote: ''Don't think only of yourself. Try to
think of the other fellow, too, and what
is best for him'' (1 Corinthians 10:24).

Quest: You give but little when you give of
your possessions. It is when you give of
yourself that you truly give (Gibran).

★

Quip: When you flee from temptation, be sure
you don't leave a forwarding address.

Quote: ''Dear brothers, is your life full of
difficulties and temptations? Then be
happy, for when the way is rough, your
patience has a chance to grow. So let it
grow, and don't try to squirm out of
your problems. For when your patience
is finally at full bloom, then you will be
ready for anything, strong in character,
full and complete'' (James 1:2-4).

Quest: Man's chief merit consists in resisting the
impulses of his nature (Johnson).

Quip: Sign tacked on a tree near a convent:
                 "No trespassing; violators will be
                 prosecuted to the fullest extent of the
                 law—Sisters of Mercy."

Quote: "Yet there is one ray of hope: his
                 compassion never ends. It is only the
                 Lord's mercies that have kept us from
                 complete destruction. Great is his
                 faithfulness; his lovingkindness begins
                 afresh each day" (Lamentations 3:21-23).

Quest: Among the attributes of God, although
                 they are all equal, mercy shines with
                 even more brilliancy than justice
                 (Cervantes).

                              ★

Quip: The more steam you put into your work,
                 the louder you can whistle when the
                 work is done.

Quote: "It is better to get your hands dirty—and
                 eat, then to be too proud to work—and
                 starve" (Proverbs 12:9).

Quest: It is better for you to wear out than to
                 rust out.

Quip: When angry, count to ten before you
               speak; if very angry count to a hundred
               (Jefferson).

Quote: ''It is better to be slow-tempered than
               famous; it is better to have self-control
               than to control an army (Proverbs
               16:32).

Quest: Anger is momentary madness, so control
               your passion or it will control you
               (Horace).

★

Quip: The fellow who has a good opinion of
               himself is likely a poor judge of human
               nature.

Quote: ''For everyone who tries to honor
               himself shall be humbled; and he who
               humbles himself shall be honored'' (Luke
               14:11).

Quest: Before retiring one evening, Theodore
               Roosevelt, gazing at the galaxies of
               stars, turned to his men and said, ''I
               believe we are now small enough to go
               to bed.''

Quip: You'll never get a hit until you get the bat off your shoulder (C.M. Ward).

Quote: "Since we have such a huge crowd of men of faith watching us from the grandstands, let us strip off anything that slows us down or holds us back, and especially those sins that wrap themselves so tightly around our feet and trip us up; and let us run with patience the particular race that God has set before us" (Hebrews 12:1).

Quest: Don't postpone reading the handwriting on the wall until you have your back to it.

★

Quip: If you think education is expensive, try ignorance (Derek Bok).

Quote: "Where there is ignorance of God, the people run wild; but what a wonderful thing it is for a nation to know and keep his laws!" (Proverbs 29:18).

Quest: Education makes a people easy to lead, but difficult to drive; easy to govern, but impossible to enslave (Lord Brougham).

Quip: If your knees are knocking, kneel on them.

Quote: "Seek the Lord; yes, seek his strength and seek his face untiringly" (1 Chronicles 16:11).

Quest: Satan trembles when he sees the weakest saint upon his knees (Cowper).

★

Quip: The Scripture passages that bother me the most are the ones I understand (Mark Twain).

Quote: "How can men be wise? The only way to begin is by reverence for God. For growth in wisdom comes from obeying his laws. Praise his name forever" (Psalm 111:10).

Quest: It is impossible to rightly govern the world without God and the Bible (Washington).

Quip: Did you hear about the undertaker who closed his letters with the words "Eventually yours"?

Quote: "And just as it is destined that men die only once, and after that comes judgment, so also Christ died only once as an offering for the sins of many people; and he will come again, but not to deal again with our sins" (Hebrews 9:27, 28).

Quest: Death is more universal than life; everyone dies but not everyone lives (Sachs).

★

Quip: Contentment is the power to get out of any situation all there is in it.

Quote: "Stay away from the love of money; be satisfied with what you have. For God has said, 'I will never fail you nor forsake you' " (Hebrews 13:5).

Quest: Every person lives in one of two "tents"—either content or discontent.

Quip: It is a pity that common sense is such an
              uncommon commodity.

Quote: "The man who strays away from
              common sense will end up dead!"
              (Proverbs 21:16).

Quest: This country is where it is today on
              account of the real common sense of
              the normal majority (Will Rogers).

                           ★

Quip: Indoor sports are all right if they go
              home at a reasonable hour.

Quote: "It is senseless for you to work so hard
              from early morning until late at night,
              fearing you will starve to death; for God
              wants his loved ones to get their proper
              rest" (Psalm 127:2).

Quest: Coach counseling his players: "Boys, you
              can't fly with the owls at night and keep
              up with the eagles in the daytime."

Quip: Some people talk not because they have something to say, but because they have to say something.

Quote: "I said to myself, I'm going to quit complaining! I'll keep quiet, especially when the ungodly are around me" (Psalm 39:1).

Quest: The ability to speak several languages is valuable, but the art of keeping silent in one is precious.

★

Quip: A curious person who asks questions may be a fool for five minutes; he who never asks questions remains a fool forever.

Quote: "And so it is with prayer—keep on asking and you will keep on getting; keep on looking and you will keep on finding; knock and the door will be opened. Everyone who asks, receives; all who seek, find; and the door is opened to everyone who knocks" (Luke 11: 9, 10).

Quest: Curiosity is simply another word for hope.

Quip: The trouble comes when the New Year's
                   resolutions collide with the old year's
                   habits.

Quote: "Can the Ethiopian change the color of
                   his skin? or a leopard take away his
                   spots? Nor can you who are so used to
                   doing evil now start being good"
                   (Jeremiah 13:23).

Quest: Habits are at first cobwebs, then cables.

                              ★

Quip: Happiness is like jam; you can't spread
                   even a little without getting some on
                   yourself.

Quote: "God blesses those who obey him;
                   happy the man who puts his trust in the
                   Lord" (Proverbs 16:20).

Quest: The thing that counts most in the pursuit
                   of happiness is choosing the right
                   traveling companion.

Quip: It's the little things in life that upset us—such as two-foot putts.

Quote: "Yes, our natural lives will fade as grass does when it becomes all brown and dry. All our greatness is like a flower that droops and falls" (1 Peter 1:24).

Quest: As you walk down the fairway of life, you must smell the roses, for you only get to play one round (Ben Hogan).

★

Quip: To a small boy, home is merely a filling station.

Quote: "These older women must train the younger women to live quietly, to love their husbands and their children, and to be sensible and clean-minded, spending their time in their own homes, being kind and obedient to their husbands, so that the Christian faith can't be spoken against by those who know them" (Titus 2:4, 5).

Quest: Home is where part of the family waits until the rest of the family brings back the car.

Quip: Regardless of policy, honesty is easier
                on the nerves.

Quote: "The night is far gone, the day of his
                return will soon be here. So quit the evil
                deeds of darkness and put on the armor
                of right living, as we who live in the
                daylight should! Be decent and true in
                everything you do so that all can
                approve your behavior. Don't spend
                your time in wild parties and getting
                drunk or in adultery and lust, or fighting,
                or jealousy" (Romans 13: 12, 13).

Quest: A shady business never yields a sunny
                life (B.C. Forbes).

★

Quip: God made man a little lower than
                angels—and he has been getting a little
                lower ever since (Will Rogers).

Quote: "I cannot understand how you can
                bother with mere puny man, to pay any
                attention to him! And yet you have
                made him only a little lower than the
                angels, and placed a crown of glory and
                honor upon his head" (Psalm 8:4,5).

Quest: To really know a man, observe his
                behavior with a woman, a flat tire, and a
                child.

Quip: A gossip is just a fool with a keen sense of rumor.

Quote: "A good man thinks before he speaks; the evil man pours out his evil words without a thought" (Proverbs 15:28).

Quest: Never tell evil of a man, if you do not know it for certainty, and if you know it for a certainty, then ask yourself, "Why should I tell it?" (Lavater).

★

Quip: Busy souls have no time to be busybodies.

Quote: "Don't let me hear of you suffering for murdering or stealing or making trouble or being a busybody and prying into other people's affairs" (1 Peter 4:15).

Quest: If for a tranquil mind you seek, these things observe with care: of whom you speak, to whom you speak, and how, and when, and where.

Quip: If you want to get into Who's Who, you
              first better find out what's what.

Quote: "Work hard so God can say to you,
              'Well done.' Be a good workman, one
              who does not need to be ashamed when
              God examines your work. Know what his
              Word says and means" (2 Timothy 2:15).

Quest: It's not the going out of port, but the
              coming in, that determines the success
              of the voyage (Beecher).

                            ★

Quip: Charity begins at home but should not
              end there.

Quote: "If I had the gift of prophecy and knew
              all about what is going to happen in the
              future, knew everything about
              everything, but didn't love others, what
              good would it do? Even if I had the gift
              of faith so that I could speak to a
              mountain and make it move, I would still
              be worth nothing at all without love"
              (1 Corinthians 13:2).

Quest: What is charity? It is silence when your
              words would hurt. It is patience when
              your neighbor's curt. It is deafness when
              a scandal flows. It is thoughtfulness for
              others' woes. It is promptness when
              stern duty calls. It is courage when
              misfortune falls.

Quip: You cannot stumble if you are on your knees.

Quote: "Pray all the time. Ask for anything in line with the Holy Spirit's wishes. Plead with him, reminding him of your needs, and keep praying earnestly for all Christians everywhere" (Ephesians 6:18).

Quest: The world seeks victory by trying to get back on its feet, the Christian by getting down on his knees.

★

Quip: Happiness is perfume that you cannot spray on others without getting a little on yourself.

Quote: "The man who knows right from wrong and has good judgment and common sense is happier than the man who is immensely rich! For such wisdom is far more valuable than precious jewels. Nothing else compares with it" (Proverbs 3:13-15).

Quest: Happiness is that peculiar sensation you acquire when you are too busy to be miserable.

Quip: He who rolls up sleeves seldom
                 loses shirt.

Quote: "A wise youth makes hay while the sun
                 shines, but what a shame to see a
                 lad who sleeps away his hour of
                 opportunity" (Proverbs 10:5).

Quest: Most of this world's useful work is done
                 by people who are pressed for time, or
                 are tired, or don't feel well.

                           ★

Quip: Children are growing up when they start
                 asking questions parents can answer.

Quote: "Teach a child to choose the right path,
                 and when he is older he will remain
                 upon it" (Proverbs 22:6).

Quest: "Sparents" are those who spare the rod
                 when offspring need attention; they find
                 their troubles multiplied in ways too sad
                 to mention.

Quip: An egotist is a person who is me-deep in conversation.

Quote: "Don't praise yourself; let others do it!" (Proverbs 27:2).

Quest: Humility is a strange thing; the moment you think you have it, you have lost it.

★

Quip: You can't get the worm out of the apple by polishing the apple.

Quote: "Yes, all have sinned; all fall short of God's glorious ideal; yet now God declares us 'not guilty' of offending him if we trust in Jesus Christ, who in his kindness freely takes away our sins" (Romans 3:23, 24).

Quest: Sin leaves a mark just as a nail leaves a hole in furniture. When you pull the nail out the hole is still there.

Quip: If at first you don't succeed, try looking
                 in the waste basket for directions.

Quote: "In everything you do, put God first,
                 and he will direct you and crown your
                 efforts with success" (Proverbs 3:6).

Quest: Did you hear about the fellow who went
                 to church to get out of his problems, but
                 all he received was directions from
                 Jerusalem to Jericho?

★

Quip: Today is the tomorrow you worried
                 about yesterday.

Quote: "So don't be anxious about tomorrow.
                 God will take care of your tomorrow
                 too. Live one day at a time"
                 (Matthew 6:34).

Quest: Worries spend a lot of time shoveling
                 smoke (Claude McDonald).

Quip: If your're not big enough to stand criticism, you're too small to be praised.

Quote: "Don't refuse to accept criticism; get all the help you can" (Proverbs 23:12).

Quest: Criticism should not be querulous and wasting, all knife and root-pulling, but guiding, instructive, inspiring—a south wind and not an east wind (Ralph Waldo Emerson).

★

Quip: The goal of Christianity is not to make *good* men but *new* men.

Quote: "When someone becomes a Christian he becomes a brand new person inside. He is not the same any more. A new life has begun" (2 Corinthians 5:17).

Quest: God loves each of us as if there were only one of us (Saint Augustine).

Quip: It's easy to be an angel when nobody ruffles your feathers.

Quote: ''Don't be misled; remember that you can't ignore God and get away with it: a man will always reap just the kind of crop he sows!'' (Galatians 6:7).

Quest: Loose conduct can quickly get you into tight places.

★

Quip: Office sign: If you have nothing to do, please don't do it here.

Quote: ''A lazy fellow has trouble all through life; the good man's path is easy!'' (Proverbs 15:19).

Quest: He slept beneath the moon, he baked beneath the sun; he lived a life of going-to-do and died with nothing done.

Quip: Never pick a quarrel even when it's ripe.

Quote: ''It is hard to stop a quarrel once it
               starts, so don't let it begin''
               (Proverbs 17:14).

Quest: The only way to get the best of an
               argument is to avoid it (Dale Carnegie).

                              ★

Quip: There are usually two sides to every
               argument but no end.

Quote: ''It is an honor for a man to stay out of
               a fight. Only fools insist on quarreling''
               (Proverbs 20:3).

Quest: Quarrels would not last long if the fault
               was only on one side (La Roche
               Foucauld).

Quip: It is better to say "This one thing I do"
              than to say "These 40 things I
              dabble in."

Quote: "No, dear brothers, I am still not all I
              should be, but I am bringing all my
              energies to bear on this one thing:
              Forgetting the past and looking forward
              to what lies ahead, I strain to reach the
              end of the race and receive the prize for
              which God is calling us up to heaven
              because of what Christ Jesus did for us"
              (Philippians 3: 13, 14).

Quest: The secret of success is constancy of
              purpose (Disraeli).

★

Quip: Did you hear about the French-horn
              player whose toupée fell into the bell of
              his horn? He spent the rest of the night
              blowing his top.

Quote: "A wise man controls his temper. He
              knows that anger causes mistakes"
              (Proverbs 14:29).

Quest: Blowing your top is no way to get up in
              the world.

Quip: None preaches better than the ant, and she says nothing (Benjamin Franklin).

Quote: "Take a lesson from the ants, you lazy fellow. Learn from their ways and be wise! For though they have no king to make them work, yet they labor hard all summer, gathering food for the winter" (Proverbs 6:6-8).

Quest: The only place where success comes before work is in the dictionary.

★

Quip: The largest room in the world is the room for improvement.

Quote: "Learn to be wise . . .and develop good judgment and common sense! I cannot overemphasize this point" (Proverbs 4:5).

Quest: Make the most of yourself with God's help, for that is all there is of you.

Quip: He who won't be counseled can't
               be helped.

Quote: "A fool thinks he needs no advice, but a
               wise men listens to others" (Proverbs
               12:15).

Quest: If you are old, give advice; if you are
               young, take it.

★

Quip: As a rule the fellow who toots his own
               horn the loudest is in the biggest fog.

Quote: "There is one thing worse than a fool,
               and that is a man who is conceited"
               (Proverbs 26:12).

Quest: Conceit may puff a man up, but never
               prop him up (Ruskin).

Quip: He who thinks by the inch and talks by the yard deserves to be kicked by the foot.

Quote: ''Search me, O God, and know my heart; test my thoughts. Point out anything you find in me that makes you sad, and lead me along the path of everlasting life'' (Psalm 139:23, 24).

Quest: Associate reverently, and as much as you can, with your loftiest thoughts (Thoreau).

★

Quip: A pastor told his congregation that there were 739 different sins. Within a week, he received 73 requests for the list.

Quote: ''But if we are living in the light of God's presence, just as Christ does, then we have wonderful fellowship and joy with each other, and the blood of Jesus his Son cleanses us from every sin. If we say that we have no sin, we are only fooling ourselves, and refusing to accept the truth. But if we confess our sins to him, he can be depended on to forgive us and to cleanse us from every wrong. (And it is perfectly proper for God to do this for us because Christ died to wash away our sins)'' (1 John 1:7-9).

Quest: Man is the only creature that blushes—or needs to.

Quip: Don't cross the bridge until you have
               the exact toll ready.

Quote: "But don't begin until you count the
               cost. For who would begin construction
               of a building without first getting
               estimates and then checking to see if he
               has enough money to pay the bills?"
               (Luke 14:28).

Quest: A Brownie leader asked her group,
               "What is the Girl Scout motto?" "Be
               repaired," piped one little miss.

                              ★

Quip: Never be dogmatic; we all make *misteaks*.

Quote: "I will instruct you (says the Lord) and
               guide you along the best pathway for
               your life; I will advise you and watch
               your progress. Don't be like a senseless
               horse or mule that has to have a bit
               in its mouth to keep it in line!"
               (Psalm 32:8, 9).

Quest: Learn from your mistakes and those of
               others. You can't live long enough to
               make them all yourself.

Quip: Prayer is the stop that keeps you going.

Quote: "Ask, and you will be given what you ask for. Seek, and you will find. Knock, and the door will be opened" (Matthew 7:7).

Quest: Don't be afraid to be honest with God; you'll never be shortchanged!

★

Quip: The first thing a girl hopes for from the garden of love is at least one carat.

Quote: "And you husbands, show the same kind of love to your wives as Christ showed to the church when he died for her" (Ephesians 5:25).

Quest: Love is oceans of emotions surrounded by expanses of expense!

Quip: He who putters around winds up in hole.

Quote: "Whatever you do, do well, for in death,
                 where you are going, there is no
                 working or planning, or knowing, or
                 understanding" (Ecclesiastes 9:10).

Quest: He started to sing as he tackled the
                 thing that couldn't be done, and he did
                 it (Edgar Guest).

★

Quip: Play every play as if it were going to be
                 the game-breaker (Vince Lombardi).

Quote: "If you won't plow in the cold, you
                 won't eat at the harvest" (Proverbs
                 20:4).

Quest: Roadside sign in Kentucky: "Pray for a
                 good harvest, but keep on hoeing."

Quip: Adversity sometimes is the only diet that
                   will reduce a fat head.

Quote: "You are a poor specimen if you can't
                   stand the pressure of adversity"
                   (Proverbs 24:10).

Quest: Adversity introduces a man to himself.

★

Quip: If you aim at nothing you're sure to
                   hit it.

Quote: "Wisdom is the main pursuit of
                   sensible men, but a fool's goals are at
                   the ends of the earth!" (Proverbs 17:24).

Quest: Your plans miscarry because they have
                   no aim. When you do not know what
                   harbor you are making for, no wind is
                   the right wind.

Quip: Mistakes will happen, but must you give them so much help?

Quote: "Love forgets mistakes; nagging about them parts the best of friends" (Proverbs 17:9).

Quest: Most people would learn from their mistakes if they weren't so busy trying to place the blame on someone else.

★

Quip: Some families think church is like a convention where you send a delegate—and it's usually Mother.

Quote: "Let us not neglect our church meetings, as some people do, but encourage and warn each other, especially now that the day of his coming back again is drawing near" (Hebrews 10:25).

Quest: A church is not a museum, an exhibition of saints, a show-ring of pious purebreds. A church is a school, a group of people in various stages of development, from beginners in the Christian life with the dirt of the world still on them to those clad in white robes of the saints.

Quip: "Whines" are the products of sour
              grapes.

Quote: "In everything you do, stay away from
              complaining and arguing, so that no one
              can speak a word of blame against you.
              You are to live clean, innocent lives as
              children of God in a dark world full of
              people who are crooked and stubborn.
              Shine out among them like beacon
              lights, holding out to them the Word
              of Life" (Philippians 2:14-16).

Quest: Sweep the snow from your own door
              before you complain of the frost on
              your neighbor's tiles.

★

Quip: If there were no God, it would have
              been necessary to invent Him (Voltaire).

Quote: "For I am convinced that nothing can
              ever separate us from his love. Death
              can't, and life can't. The angels won't,
              and all the power of hell itself cannot
              keep God's love away (Romans 8:38).

Quest: My concern is not whether God is on
              our side; my great concern is to be on
              God's side, for God is always right
              (Lincoln).

Quip: A hangover is the moaning after the
               night before.

Quote: "Don't let the sparkle and the smooth
               taste of wine deceive you . . .You will
               see hallucinations and have delirium
               tremens, and you will say foolish, silly
               things that would embarrass you at no
               end when sober" (Proverbs 23:31, 33).

Quest: Wife to husband with a hangover: "I
               don't see why your head should hurt
               this morning—you certainly didn't use it
               last night."

                              ★

Quip: Home is where we were treated the best
               and grumble the most.

Quote: "She gets up before dawn to prepare
               breakfast for her household, and plans
               the day's work for her servant
               girls . . .She is energetic, a hard worker,
               and watches for bargains. She works far
               into the night!"(Proverbs 31: 15, 17, 18).

Quest: A hundred men can make an
               encampment, but it requires a woman
               to make a home.

Quip: To stay out of hot water, keep a
cool head.

Quote: "It is better to be slow-tempered than
famous; it is better to have self-control
than to control an army" (Proverbs
16:32).

Quest: There is little that can withstand a man
who can conquer himself.

★

Quip: Blessed is he who expects nothing, for
he shall never be disappointed.

Quote: "Hope deferred makes a heart sick; but
when dreams come true at last, there is
life and joy" (Proverbs 13:12).

Quest: Disappointment should always be taken
as a stimulant, and never viewed as a
discouragement.

Quip: A brook would lose its song if it had no rocks.

Quote: "Fight on for God. Hold tightly to the eternal life which God has given you, and which you have confessed with such a ringing confession before many witnesses" (1 Timothy 6:12).

Quest: The person who has not struggled with difficulty after difficulty cannot know the joy of genuine success. Face the problems and fight your way over them. There is more satisfaction in putting forth effort than in gloating over easily won profits. The rungs in the ladder of success are composed of difficulties.

★

Quip: Church members, like autos, usually start missing before they quit.

Quote: "And let us not get tired of what is right, for after a while we will reap a harvest of blessing if we don't get discouraged and give up. That's why whenever we can we should always be kind to everyone, and especially to our Christian brothers" (Galatians 6:9, 10).

Quest: The world at its worst needs the church at its best.

Quip: Remember, people will judge you by your actions, not your intentions. You may have a heart of gold—but so does a hard-boiled egg.

Quote: ''A good man produces good deeds from a good heart. And an evil man produces evil deeds from his hidden wickedness. Whatever is in the heart overflows into speech'' (Luke 6:45).

Quest: What is in the well of your heart will show up in the bucket of your speech.

★

Quip: When God measures a man, He puts the tape around the heart instead of the head.

Quote: ''If your profits are in heaven your heart will be there too'' (Matthew 6:21).

Quest: In judging others it's always best to see with the heart as well as the eyes.

Quip: The smile that lights the face will also
              warm the heart.

Quote: "A happy face means a glad heart; a sad
              face means a breaking heart"
              (Proverbs 15:13).

Quest: Sympathy is the result of thinking with
              your heart.

★

Quip: A smile is God's cosmetic.

Quote: "A cheerful heart does good like
              medicine, but a broken spirit makes one
              sick" (Proverbs 17:22).

Quest: Why not wear a smile? It's just about the
              only thing you can wear that isn't taxed.

Quip: If there is no hell, a good many preachers are obtaining money under false pretenses (Billy Sunday).

Quote: "The wicked shall be sent away to hell; this is the fate of all the nations forgetting the Lord" (Psalm 9:17).

Quest: The road to hell is paved with good intentions (Johnson).

★

Quip: So live that when death comes the mourners will outnumber the cheering section.

Quote: "If you must choose, take a good name rather than great riches; for to be held in loving esteem is better than silver and gold" (Proverbs 22:1).

Quest: Associate yourself with men of good quality if you esteem your own reputation, for it is better to be alone than in bad company (Washington).

Quip: If all of us hang our troubles on a clothesline, most of us would choose our own troubles.

Quote: "Mankind heads for sin and misery as predictably as flames shoot upwards from a fire" (Job 5:7).

Quest: Troubles bind people together.

★

Quip: The hardest thing to give is in.

Quote: "And even though Jesus was God's Son, he had to learn from experience what it was like to obey, when obeying meant suffering" (Hebrews 5:8).

Quest: Christ was one child who knew more than His parents—yet He submitted to them.

Quip: Your personal liberty ends where my nose begins.

Quote: "For, dear brothers, you have been given freedom: not freedom to do wrong, but freedom to love and serve each other" (Galatians 5:13).

Quest: Freedom is not a question of doing as we like but doing as we ought.

★

Quip: The worst thing about history is that every time it repeats itself the price goes up.

Quote: " 'I am the A and the Z, the Beginning and the Ending of all things,' says God, who is the Lord, the All Powerful One who is, and was, and is coming again!" (Revelations 1:8).

Quest: Christ is the eternal fact in the world's history; to Him everything looks forward or backward (Spurgeon).

Quip: Every day God makes silk purses out of sows' ears.

Quote: "Now glory be to God who by his mighty power at work within us is able to do far more than we would ever dare to ask or even dream of—infinitely beyond our highest prayers, desires, thoughts, or hopes" (Ephesians 3:20).

Quest: God moves in mysterious ways His wonders to perform; He plants His footsteps in the sea, and rides upon the storm (Cowper).

★

Quip: When the will is ready the feet are light.

Quote: "So, dear brothers, you have no obligations whatever to your old sinful nature to do what it begs you to do. For if you keep on following it you are lost and will perish, but if through the power of the Holy Spirit you crush it and its evil deeds, you shall live" (Romans 8:12, 13).

Quest: If your will power doesn't work, try your "won't" power.

Quip: A good deal of trouble has been caused in the world by too much intelligence and too little wisdom.

Quote: "Determination to be wise is the first step toward becoming wise! And with your wisdom, develop common sense and good judgment" (Proverbs 4:7).

Quest: Wisdom is knowing what to do next, skill is knowing how to do it, and virtue is doing it (David Starr Jordan).

★

Quip: Silence is golden except when it comes to witnessing—then it's just plain yellow.

Quote: "But when the Holy Spirit has come upon you, you will receive power to testify about me with great effect, to the people of Jerusalem, throughout Judea, in Samaria, and to the ends of the earth, about my death and resurrection" (Acts 1:8).

Quest: If you want your neighbor to know what the Lord will do for him, let him see and hear what He has done for you.

Quip: Whenever you're in doubt, faith it.

Quote: "You can never please God without
                 faith, without depending on him. Anyone
                 who wants to come to God must believe
                 that there is a God and that he rewards
                 those who sincerely look for him"
                 (Hebrews 11:6).

Quest: Faith takes up the cross, love binds it to
                 the soul, and patience bears it to the
                 end.

                          ★

Quip: Courage is fear that has said its prayers.

Quote: "With them on guard you can sleep
                 without fear; you need not be afraid of
                 disaster or the plots of wicked men, for
                 the Lord is with you; he protects you"
                 (Proverbs 3:24-26).

Quest: Bravery never goes out of fashion
                 (Thackeray).

Quip: A warm smile thaws an icy stare.

Quip: "A happy face means a glad heart; a
                sad face means a breaking heart"
                (Proverbs 15:13).

Quest: A smile is the lighting system of the face
                and the heating system of the heart.

                                ★

Quip: The curve of a smile can set a lot of
                things straight.

Quote: "A cheerful heart does good like
                medicine, but a broken spirit makes one
                sick" (Proverbs 17:22).

Quest: What sunshine is to flowers, smiles are
                to humanity (Addison).

Quip: Even if you're on the right track, you'll
               get run over if you just sit there.

Quote: "Since we have such a huge crowd of
               men of faith watching us from the grand-
               stands, let us strip off anything that
               slows us down or holds us back, and
               especially those sins that wrap
               themselves so tightly around our feet
               and trip us up; and let us run with
               patience the particular race that God has
               set before us. Keep your eyes on Jesus,
               our leader and instructor"
               (Hebrews 12:1, 2).

Quest: Here are five keys to fulfillment: Obey
               the great God; dream great dreams; plan
               great plans; pray great prayers; claim
               great victories.

                          ★

Quip: A mistake is proof that somebody tried
               anyhow.

Quote: "A man who refuses to admit his
               mistakes can never be successful. But if
               he confesses and forsakes them, he gets
               another chance" (Proverbs 28:13).

Quest: The greatest mistake you can make in
               this life is to be continually fearing you
               will make one (Hubbard).

Quip: The most underdeveloped territory in the world lies under your hat.

Quote: "He wrote them to teach his people how to live—how to act in every circumstance, for he wanted them to be understanding, just and fair in everything they did . . .I want those already wise to become the wiser and become leaders by exploring the depths of meaning in these nuggets of truth" (Proverbs 1:2, 3, 5, 6).

Quest: I use not only all the brains I have, but all I can borrow (Woodrow Wilson).

★

Quip: Christians may not always see eye-to-eye, but they can walk arm-in-arm.

Quote: "How wonderful it is, how pleasant, when brothers live in harmony! For harmony is as precious as the fragrant anointing of oil that was poured over Aaron's head, and ran down his beard, and onto the border of his robe. Harmony is as refreshing as the dew on Mount Hermon, on the mountains of Israel" (Psalm 133:1-3).

Quest: United we stand, divided we fall.

Quip: She was noted for her position in the
              meddle class.

Quote: "This should be your ambition: to live a
              quiet life, minding your own business
              and doing your own work, just as we
              told you before" (1 Thessalonians 4:11).

Quest: One of the hardest things about
              business is minding your own.

                           ★

Quip: When he meets another egotist, it's an I
              for an I. Really, they are both I-sores.

Quote: "As God's messenger I give each of you
              God's warning: Be honest in your
              estimate of yourselves, measuring your
              value by how much faith God has given
              you" (Romans 12:3).

Quest: One of the hardest secrets for man to
              keep is his opinion of himself.

Quip: Horse sense is stable thinking coupled with the ability to say nay.

Quote   "Get the facts at any price, and hold on tightly to all the good sense you can get" (Proverbs 23:23).

Quest   Common sense is seeing things as they are, and doing things as they should be done.

★

Quip   Good conversation, like a defensive driver, yields the right of way (DeBolt).

Quote   "Make the most of your chances to tell others the Good News. Be wise in all your contacts with them. Let your conversation be gracious as well as sensible, for then you will have the right answer for everyone" (Colossians 4:5, 6).

Quest   A good listener is not only popular everywhere, but after a while he knows something (Misner).

Quip: He who rides a tiger cannot dismount.

Quote: "Under the laws of Moses the rule was,
               'If you kill, you must die.' But I have
               added to that rule, and tell you that if
               you are only angry, even in your own
               home, you are in danger of judgment! If
               you call your friend an idiot, you are in
               danger of being brought before the
               court. And if you curse him, you are in
               danger of the fires of hell" (Matthew
               5:21, 22).

Quest: The most dangerous thing in the world is
               to try to leap a chasm in two jumps
               (Lloyd-George).

                              ★

Quip: Girls who associate with punks should
               expect fireworks.

Quote: "Be with wise men and become wise. Be
               with evil men and become evil"
               (Proverbs 13:20).

Quest: The biggest worry of a doting father is a
               dating daughter.

Quip: Almost everyone knows the difference
              between right and wrong; some people
              just have to make decisions.

Quote: "But if you are unwilling to obey the
              Lord, then decide today whom you will
              obey. Will it be the gods of your
              ancestors beyond the Euphrates or the
              gods of the Amorites here in this land?
              But as for me and my family, we will
              serve the Lord" (Joshua 24:15).

Quest: Please, never make a decision based on
              fear.

                        ★

Quip: He who has sharp tongue usually cuts
              own throat.

Quote: "Self-control means controlling the
              tongue! A quick retort can ruin
              everything" (Proverbs 13:3).

Quest: A sharp tongue is the only edged tool
              that grows keener with constant use
              (Irving).

Quip: When you became a Christian, God didn't call you to a playground but a battleground.

Quote: "Last of all I want to remind you that your strength must come from the Lord's mighty power within you. Put on all of God's armor so that you will be able to stand safe against all strategies and tricks of Satan" (Ephesians 6:10, 11).

Quest: God gets His best soldiers out of the highlands of affliction (Spurgeon).

★

Quip: Did you hear about the fellow who climbed the ladder of success wrong by wrong?

Quote: "Now glory be to God who by his mighty power at work within us is able to do far more than we would ever dare to ask or even dream of—infinitely beyond our highest prayers, desires, thoughts, or hopes" (Ephesians 3:20).

Quest: The rung of a ladder was never meant to rest upon, but only to hold a man's foot long enough to enable him to put the other foot somewhat higher (Huxley).

Quip: Take your stand! If you don't stand for
               something you'll fall for everything.

Quote: "So use every piece of God's armor to
               resist the enemy whenever he attacks,
               and when it is all over, you will still be
               standing up" (Ephesians 6:13).

Quest: Are you sitting on the premises or
               standing on the promises?

                            ★

Quip: People who gossip usually wind up in
               their own mouth traps.

Quote: "Fire goes out for a lack of fuel, and
               tensions disappear when gossip
               stops . . .Gossip is a dainty morsel eaten
               with great relish" (Proverbs 26:20,22).

Quest: A gossip is a person who jumps to a
               conclusion, takes people at deface
               value, and knows how to add to and to.

Quip: Sin will keep you from the Bible, but the
                 Bible will keep you from sin.

Quote: "How can a young man stay pure? By
                 reading your Word and following its
                 rules. I have tried my best to find
                 you—don't let me wander off from your
                 instructions. I have thought much about
                 your words, and stored them in my
                 heart so that they would hold me back
                 from sin" (Psalm 119:9-11).

Quest: The Bible is a window in this prison-
                 world through which we may look into
                 eternity.

★

Quip: No one wants to be brave anymore—
                 just chief!

Quote: "Be strong! Be courageous! Do not be
                 afraid of them! For the Lord your God
                 will be with you. He will neither fail you
                 nor forsake you" (Deuteronomy 31:6).

Quest: When moral courage feels that it is in
                 the right, there is no personal daring of
                 which it is incapable (Hunt).

Quip: Aim high but stay on the level.

Quote: "Happy is the man with a level-headed son; sad the mother of a rebel" (Proverbs 10:1).

Quest: Hitch your wagon to the stars but keep your feet on the ground.

★

Quip: Cooperate! Remember the banana. Every time it leaves the bunch it gets skinned.

Quote: "Apollos and I are working as a team, with the same aim, though each of us will be rewarded for his own hard work. We are only God's co-workers. You are God's garden, not ours; you are God's building, not ours" (1 Corinthians 3:8,9).

Quest: Act like a heel toward teammates and you'll get walked on.

Quip: Thomas Edison said, "Genius is about 2 percent inspiration and 98 percent perspiration."

Quote: "Do you know a hard-working man? He shall be successful and stand before kings." (Proverbs 22:29).

Quest: An efficiency expert is someone who is smart enough to tell you how to run your business and too smart to start one of his own.

★

Quip: Christians may not always see eye-to-eye, but they can walk arm-in-arm.

Quote: "How wonderful it is, how pleasant, when brothers live in harmony! For harmony is as precious as the fragrant anointing of oil that was poured over Aaron's head, and ran down onto his beard, and onto the border of his robe. Harmony is as refreshing as the dew on Mount Hermon, on the mountains of Israel" (Psalm 133:1-3).

Quest: United we stand, divided we fall.

Quip: Life is like playing a violin solo in public and learning the instrument as one goes on (Bulwer-Lytton).

Quote: "God gave these four youths great ability to learn, and they soon mastered all the literature and science of the time; and God gave to Daniel special ability in understanding the meanings of dreams and visions" (Daniel 1:17).

Quest: We have to learn to swim under water like fish; we have learned to fly through the air like birds; all we have to do now is learn to walk this earth like men.

★

Quip: Sign on Ronald Reagan's desk: "There is no limit to what a man can do or where he can go if he doesn't mind who gets the credit."

Quote: "Keep your eyes on Jesus, our leader and instructor. He was willing to die a shameful death on the cross because of the joy he knew would be his afterwards; and now he sits in the place of honor by the throne of God" (Hebrews 12:2).

Quest: Fortunate is the person who has learned that the most certain way to "get" is to first "give" through some sort of useful service.

Quip: If you're going to poke your head above
              the crowd, you may as well expect
              tomatoes. If you get them, make ketchup
              (Jim Bakker).

Quote: "I will be staying here at Ephesus until
              the holiday of Pentecost, for there is a
              wide open door for me to preach and
              teach here. So much is happening, but
              there are many enemies" (1 Corinthians
              16:8,9).

Quest: He knows not his own strength who hath
              not met adversity. Heaven prepares
              good men with crosses (Johnson).

                          ★

Quip: Honor lies in honest toil (Cleveland).

Quote: "Dear brothers, honor the officers of
              your church who work hard among you
              and warn you against all that is wrong.
              Think highly of them and give them your
              wholehearted love because they are
              straining to help you" (1 Thessalonians
              5:12,13).

Quest: I feel it is time that I also pay tribute to
              my four writers (Matthew, Mark, Luke,
              and John (Bishop Sheen).

Quip: Silence is evidence of a superb
              command of the English language.

Quote: "There is a right time for everything . . .a
              time to tear; a time to repair; a time to
              be quiet; a time to speak up"
              (Ecclesiastes 3:1,7).

Quest: I regret often that I have spoken; never
              that I have been silent (Syrus).

★

Quip: Speak when you are angry and you'll
              make the best speech you'll ever regret.

Quote: "A wise man restrains his anger and
              overlooks insults. This is to his credit"
              (Proverbs 19:11).

Quest: Whenever you are angry, be assured
              that it is not only a present evil, but that
              you have increased a habit (Epictetus).

Quip: Success that goes to your head usually
               pays a short visit.

Quote: "Pride goes before destruction and
               haughtiness before a fall. Better poor
               and humble than proud and rich"
               (Proverbs 16:18,19).

Quest: Isn't it a shame that when success turns
               someone's head it doesn't wring his
               neck at the same time!

                        ★

Quip: The man who never makes a mistake
               works for the man who does.

Quote: "Admit your faults to one another and
               pray for each other so that you may be
               healed. The earnest prayer of a
               righteous man has great power and
               wonderful results" (James 5:16).

Quest: Most people would learn from their
               mistakes if they weren't so busy trying
               to place the blame on someone else.

Quip: Happiness is a rebound from hard work.

Quote: "But happy is the man who has the God
of Jacob as his helper, whose hope is in
the Lord his God—the God who made
both earth and heaven, the seas and
everything in them. He is the God who
keeps every promise" (Psalm 146:5,6).

Quest: All who joy would win must share
it—happiness was born a twin.

★

Quip: Success comes in cans; failure comes in
can'ts.

Quote: "For I can do everything God asks me to
with the help of Christ who gives me the
strength and power" (Philippians 4:13).

Quest: Success for you is largely hanging on
after others have let go, getting up one
more time than falling down.

Quip: An error gracefully acknowledged is a
              victory won (Gascoigne).

Quote: "If we say we have no sin, we are only
              fooling ourselves, and refusing to accept
              the truth. But if we confess our sins to
              him, he can be depended on to forgive
              us and to cleanse us from every wrong.
              (And it is perfectly proper for God to do
              this for us because Christ died to wash
              away our sins) (1 John 1:8,9).

Quest: Any man worth his salt will stick up for
              what he believes is right, but it takes a
              slightly bigger man to acknowledge
              instantly and without reservation that he
              is in error.

                          ★

Quip: It is manlike to punish but Godlike to
              forgive (Winter).

Quote: "Give us our food again today, as usual,
              and forgive us our sins, just as we have
              forgiven those who have sinned against
              us" (Matthew 6:11,12).

Quest: You have a tremendous advantage over
              the person who slanders you or does
              you a willful injustice; you have it within
              your power to forgive that person.

Quip: Experience is a hard teacher. She gives the test first, the lessons afterward.

Quote: "You are my hiding place from every storm of life; you even keep me from getting into trouble! You surround me with songs of victory. I will instruct you (says the Lord) and guide you along the best pathway for your life; I will advise you and watch your progress" (Psalm 32:7,8).

Quest: I have but one lamp by which my feet are guided, and that is the lamp of experience (Henry).

★

Quip: We have forty million reasons for failure, but not a single excuse (Kipling).

Quote: "Since earliest times men have seen the earth and sky and all God made, and have known of his existence and great eternal power. So they will have no excuse (when they stand before God at Judgment Day)" (Romans 1:20).

Quest: A failure is a man who has blundered but is not able to cash in on the experience (Hubbard).

Quip: To be the picture of health, be in a good frame of mind.

Quote: "He will keep in perfect peace all those who trust in him, whose thoughts turn often to the Lord! Trust in the Lord God always, for in the Lord Jehovah is your everlasting strength" (Isaiah 26:3,4).

Quest: The true, strong, and sound mind is the mind that can equally embrace great things and small (Johnson).

★

Quip: I like work; it fascinates me. I can sit and look at it for hours. I love to keep it by me: The idea of getting rid of it nearly breaks my heart (Jerome).

Quote: "Work brings profit; talk brings poverty" (Proverbs 14:23).

Quest: I never did anything worth doing by accident, nor did any of my inventions come by accident; they came by work (Edison).

Quip: Learn from the skillful: He who teaches
                himself has a fool for a master.

Quote: "How does a man become wise? The
                first step is to trust and reverence the
                Lord! Only fools refuse to be taught.
                Listen to your father and mother. What
                you learn from them will stand you in
                good stead; it will gain you many
                honors" (Proverbs 1:7-9).

Quest: Reading maketh a full man, conference a
                ready man, and writing an exact man
                (Bacon).

★

Quip: The best way to test a man's friendship
                is to ask him to go on your note. If he
                refuses, he is your friend.

Quote: "It is poor judgment to countersign
                another's note; to become responsible
                for his debts" (Proverbs 17:18).

Quest: Be slow to fall into friendship, but when
                thou art in, continue firm and constant
                (Socrates).

Quip: Sign over college classroom clock:
              "Time will pass—will you?"

Quote: "The Lord hates cheating and delights in
              honesty" (Proverbs 11:1).

Quest: Unfaithfulness in the keeping of an
              appointment is an act of clear dishones-
              ty. You may as well borrow a person's
              money as his time (Mann).

                         ★

Quip: There's only a slight difference between
              keeping your chin up and sticking your
              neck out, but it's a difference worth
              knowing.

Quote: "But whatever happens to me,
              remember always to live as Christians
              should, so that, whether I ever see you
              again or not, I will keep on hearing good
              reports that you are standing side by
              side with one strong purpose—to tell the
              Good News fearlessly, no matter what
              your enemies may do. They will see this
              as a sign of their downfall, but for you it
              will be a clear sign from God that he is
              with you, and that he has given you eter-
              nal life with him" (Philippians 1:27,28).

Quest: It is easy to be brave from a safe
              distance (Aesop).

Quip: We have two ears and only one tongue in order that we may hear more and speak less (Diogenes).

Quote: "And so, young men, listen to me, for how happy are all who follow my instructions. Listen to my counsel—oh, don't refuse it—and be wise" (Proverbs 8:32,33).

Quest: Know how to listen, and you will profit even from those who talk badly (Plutarch).

★

Quip: An optimist is a fellow who double-parks outside a store while his wife steps into the store for a "moment."

Quote: "There is a right time for everything" (Ecclesiastes 3:1).

Quest: I recommend you take care of the minutes, for the hours will take care of themselves (Chesterfield).

Quip: The "man of the hour" never watches
          the clock.

Quote: "Read the history books and see—for we
          were born but yesterday and know so
          little; our days here on earth are as
          transient as shadows. But the wisdom of
          the past will teach you. The experience
          of others will speak to you" (Job 8:8-10).

Quest: Know the true value of time; snatch,
          seize, and enjoy every moment of it. No
          idleness, no laziness, no procrastination:
          Never put off till tomorrow what you can
          do today (Chesterfield).

                           ★

Quip: Give yourself to God; He can do more
          with you than you can.

Quote: "And so, dear brothers, I plead with you
          to give your bodies to God. Let them be
          a living sacrifice, holy—the kind he can
          accept. When you think of what he has
          done for you, is this too much to ask?
          Don't copy the behavior and customs of
          this world, but be a new and different
          person with a fresh newness in all you
          do and think. Then you will learn from
          your own experience how his ways will
          really satisfy you" (Romans 12:1,2).

Quest: If my hand slacked, I should rob
          God—since He is fullest good—leaving a
          blank instead of violins. He could not
          make Antonio Stradivarius' violins
          without Antonio (Mary Ann Evans).

Quip: Tart words make no friends; a spoonful of honey will catch more flies than a gallon of vinegar.

Quote: "Some people like to make cutting remarks, but the words of the wise soothe and heal" (Proverbs 12:18).

Quest: If someone were to pay you ten cents for every kind word you spoke about people, and collect five cents for every unkind word, would you be rich or poor?

★

Quip: Men occasionally stumble over the truth, but most of them pick themselves up, and hurry off as if nothing had happened.

Quote: "Anyone who leads a blameless life and is truly sincere. Anyone who refuses to slander others, does not listen to gossip, never harms his neighbor, speaks out against sin, criticizes those commiting it, commends the faithful followers of the Lord, keeps his promise even if it ruins him, does not crush his debtors with high interest rates, and refuses to testify against the innocent despite the bribes offered him—such a man shall stand firm forever" (Psalm 15:2-5).

Quest: Those who never retract their opinions love themselves more than they love truth.

Quip: National Pickle Week and Mother's Day are both in May. Isn't it strange that we devote 24 hours a year honoring mothers and seven days celebrating a relish?

Quote: "If you can find a truly good wife, she is worth more than precious gems! . . .Her children stand and bless her; so does her husband. He praises her with these words: 'There are many fine women in the world, but you are the best of them all!' " (Proverbs 31:10,28,29).

Quest: All that I am or hope to be, I owe to my angel mother (Lincoln).

★

Quip: God must have loved the plain people: He made so many of them (Lincoln).

Quote: "Shout with joy before the Lord, O earth! Obey him gladly; come before him, singing with joy. Try to realize what this means—the Lord is God! He made us—we are his people, the sheep of his pasture" (Psalm 100:1-3).

Quest: There are three kinds of people in all types of organizations—rowboat people, sailboat people, and steamboat people. Rowboat people need to be pushed or shoved along. Sailboat people move when a favorable wind is blowing. Steamboat people move continuously, through calm or storm. They are usually masters of themselves, their surroundings, and their destination.

Quip: Some people who think they are
                dreamers are just sleepers.

Quote: "If you love sleep, you will end in poverty.
                Stay awake, work hard, and there will be
                plenty to eat!" (Proverbs 20:13).

Quest: The degree of vision that dwells in a
                man is a correct measure of the man
                (Carlyle).

                            ★

Quip: Politics is becoming a precarious game.
                One week a politician may appear on
                the cover of Time, and the next week he
                may be serving it.

Quote: "Here are my directions: Pray much for
                others; plead for God's mercy upon
                them; give thanks for all he is going to
                do for them. Pray in this way for kings
                and all others who are in authority over
                us, or are in places of high responsibility,
                so that we can live in peace and
                quieteness, spending our time in godly
                living and thinking much about the
                Lord" (1 Timothy 2:1,2).

Quest: A politician thinks of the next election; a
                statesman, of the next generation
                (Clarke).

Quip: A pessimist is a person who looks at the world through woes-colored glasses (Colmes).

Quote: "That is what is meant by the Scriptures which say that no mere man has ever seen, heard or even imagined what wonderful things God has ready for those who love the Lord" (1 Corinthians 2:9).

Quest: Your future is as bright as the promises of God.

★

Quip: Some men wake up to find themselves famous; others stay up all night and become notorious.

Quote: "If you must choose, take a good name rather than great riches; for to be held in loving esteem is better than silver or gold" (Proverbs 22:1).

Quest: There are two very difficult things in the world. One is to make a name for oneself and the other is to keep it (Schumann).

Quip: Politeness is the art of choosing among your thoughts.

Quote: "But to obtain these gifts, you need more than faith; you must also work hard to be good, and even that is not enough. For then you must learn to know God better and discover what he wants you to do. Next, learn to put aside your own desires so that you will become patient and godly, gladly letting God have his way with you. This will make possible the next step, which is for you to enjoy other people and to like them, and finally you will grow to love them deeply" (2 Peter 1:5-7).

Quest: One day on a bus, a man gave his seat to a woman. She fainted. Upon recovering, she thanked him. Then he fainted.

★

Quip: A political war: one in which everyone shoots from the lip.

Quote: "Don't talk so much. You keep putting your foot in your mouth. Be sensible and turn off the flow! When a good man speaks, he is worth listening to, but the words of fools are a dime a dozen" (Proverbs 10:19,20).

Quest: Adlai Stevenson once said that a politician is a person who approaches a question with an open mouth.

Quip: If doubt overtakes you, stop for a faith
               lift.

Quote: "Yet faith comes from listening to this
               Good News—the Good News about
               Christ" (Romans 10:17).

Quest: Doubt sees the obstacles, faith sees the
               way; doubt sees the darkest night, faith
               sees the day; doubt dreads to take a
               step, faith soars on high; doubt
               questions "Who believes?" while faith
               answers "I".

                           ★

Quip: If it weren't for the optimist the
               pessimist would never know how happy
               he isn't.

Quote: "How thankful I am to Christ Jesus our
               Lord for choosing me as one of his
               messengers, and giving me the strength
               to be faithful to him" (1 Timothy 1:12).

Quest: An optimist may be wrong, but he bears
               mistakes with fortitude.

Quip: He who lacks courage thinks with his
              legs.

Quote: "Don't be impatient. Wait for the Lord,
              and he will come and save you! Be
              brave, stouthearted and courageous.
              Yes, wait and he will help you"
              (Psalm 27:14).

Quest: One person with courage makes a
              majority.

★

Quip: There are obviously two educations:
              One should teach us how to make a
              living, and the other how to live
              (Adams).

Quote: "How does a man become wise? The
              first step is to trust and reverence the
              Lord! Only fools refuse to be taught.
              Listen to your father and mother. What
              you learn from them will stand you in
              good stead; it will gain you many
              honors" (Proverbs 1:7-9).

Quest: All successful men have an education.
              Some got it without going to school and
              some got it after going to school.

Quip: Faith is not a pill you take but a muscle
                   you use.

Quote: "What is faith? It is the confident
                   assurance that something we want is
                   going to happen. It is the certainty that
                   what we hope for is waiting for us, even
                   though we cannot see it up ahead"
                   (Hebrews 11:1).

Quest: Faith must be dead to doubt, dumb to
                   discouragement, and blind to
                   impossibilities; it must know nothing but
                   success. To the believer, desire plus
                   faith minus doubt equals the answer.

                                   ★

Quip: You are only young once, but you can
                   stay immature indefinitely.

Quote: "Let us stop going over the same old
                   ground again and again, always teaching
                   those first lessons about Christ. Let us
                   go on instead to other things and
                   become mature in our understanding, as
                   strong Christians ought to be" (Hebrews
                   6:1).

Quest: To exist is to change, to change is to
                   mature, to mature is to go on creating
                   oneself endlessly.

Quip: Only a mediocre person is always at his best.

Quote: "In a race, everyone runs but only one person gets first prize. So run your race to win" (1 Corinthians 9:24).

Quest: Mediocrity is a sin. Don't do your bit; do your best (Admiral "Bull" Halsey).

★

Quip: Like a parachute, your mind only functions when it's open.

Quote: "Then make me truly happy by loving each other and agreeing wholeheartedly with each other, working together with one heart and mind and purpose" (Philippians 2:2).

Quest: Making up your mind is like making a bed. It usually helps to have someone on the other side.

Quip: The only time most of us hear money talking is when it's doing a countdown before taking off.

Quote: ''Riches can disappear fast. And the king's crown doesn't stay in his family forever—so watch your business interests closely. Know the state of your flocks and your herds'' (Proverbs 27:23,24).

Quest: Money may talk, but have you ever noticed how hard of hearing it is when you call it?

★

Quip: Missionary work is simply one beggar telling another where to find bread.

Quote: ''And then he told them, 'You are to go into all the world and preach the Good News to everyone, everywhere' '' (Mark 16:15).

Quest: A missionary is God's man, in God's place, doing God's work, in God's way, for God's glory.

Quip: The man who invented the eraser had the human race pretty well sized up.

Quote: "Dear brothers, if a Christian is overcome by some sin, you who are godly should gently and humbly help him back onto the right path, remembering that next time it might be one of you who is in the wrong . . .Each of us must bear some faults and burdens of his own. For none of us is perfect" (Galatians 6:1,5).

Quest: To err is human, but when the eraser wears out long before the pencil, don't you think you're overdoing it?

★

Quip: By the time a man discovers that money doesn't grow on trees, he's already out on a limb.

Quote: "Don't weary yourself trying to get rich. Why waste your time? For riches can disappear as though they had the wings of a bird!" (Proverbs 23:4,5).

Quest: Even if money did grow on trees, some people wouldn't shake a limb to get it.

Quip: A dollar may not go as far as it used to, but what it lacks in distance it makes up in speed.

Quote: "If you love sleep, you will end in poverty. Stay awake, work hard, and there will be plenty to eat!" (Proverbs 20:13).

Quest: The best way to hear money jingle in your pocket is to "shake a leg."

★

Quip: Things that once brought disgrace now bring a movie, a book, or a television contract.

Quote: "Godliness exalts a nation, but sin is reproach to any people" (Proverbs 14:34).

Quest: If history teaches one lesson above another, it is that leadership passes from nations whose morals become corrupt.

Quip: Horse sense shows itself when a fellow knows enough to stay away from a nag.

Quote: "It is better to live in the corner of an attic than with a crabby woman in a lovely home" (Proverbs 21:9).

Quest: Common sense is the knack of seeing things as they are, and doing things as they ought to be done (Stowe).

★

Quip: Some people go about doing good; other people just go about.

Quote: "The lazy man longs for many things but his hands refuse to work. He is greedy to get, while the godly love to give!" (Proverbs 21:25, 26).

Quest: There are at least four things you can do with your hands: You can wring them in despair, you can fold them in idleness, you can clench them in anger, or you can put them to some useful task.

Quip: Hats off to the past, sleeves up for the
             future.

Quote: "A prudent man foresees the difficulties
             ahead and prepares for them; the
             simpleton goes blindly on and suffers
             the consequences" (Proverbs 22:3).

Quest: The past is valuable to you as a
             guidepost, but dangerous if used as a
             hitching-post.

★

Quip: Wealthy people miss one of life's
             greatest pleasures—paying the last
             installment.

Quote: "Happy is the man who doesn't give in
             and do wrong when he is tempted, for
             afterwards he will get as his reward the
             crown of life that God has promised
             those who love him" (James 1:12).

Quest: Consider the postage stamp. It secures
             success through its ability to stick to one
             thing till it gets there (Billings).

Quip: If you could kick the person responsible
              for most of your troubles, you wouldn't
              be able to sit down for six months.

Quote: "God is our refuge and strength,
              a tested help in times of trouble"
              (Psalm 46:1).

              "I want you to trust me in your times of
              trouble, so I can rescue you, and you
              can give me glory" (Psalm 50:15).

Quest: The best way to meet trouble is to face
              it.

★

Quip: The lazier a man is, the more he plans
              to do tomorrow.

Quote: "Don't brag about your plans for
              tomorrow—wait and see what happens
              (Proverbs 27:1).

Quest: Yesterday is gone; forget it! Tomorrow
              never comes; don't wait for it! Today is
              here; use it!

Quip: Beware of a half-truth; you may get hold
                    of the wrong half.

Quote: "But I was born a sinner, yes, from the
                    moment my mother conceived me. You
                    deserve honesty from the heart; yes,
                    utter sincerity and truthfulness. Oh, give
                    me this wisdom" (Psalm 51:5, 6).

Quest: The greatest homage we can pay to
                    truth is to use it (Emerson).

                              ★

Quip: Tact is the ability to shut your mouth
                    before someone else wants to.

Quote: "We try to live in such a way that no
                    one will ever be offended or kept back
                    from finding the Lord by the way we act,
                    so that no one can find fault with us and
                    blame it on the Lord" (2 Corinthians
                    6:3).

Quest: Tact is the ability to put your best foot
                    forward without stepping on anyone's
                    toes.

Quip: He who growls all day lives a dog's life.

Quote: "In everything you do, stay away from complaining and arguing, so that no one can speak a word of blame against you" (Philippians 2:14,15).

Quest: There are two "dogs" inside you—the old dog (old life) and the new dog (Christian life). The dog that wins is the one you feed.

★

Quip: Today's mighty oak is just yesterday's nut that held its ground.

Quote: "And let us not get tired of doing what is right, for after a while we will reap a harvest of blessing if we don't get discouraged and give up" (Galatians 6:9).

Quest: No person in the world has more determination than he who can stop after eating one peanut.

Quip: He who cannot stand the heat should
                 stay out of the kitchen.

Quote: "If you profit from constructive criticism
                 you will be elected to the wise men's
                 hall of fame. But to reject criticism is to
                 harm yourself and your own best
                 interests" (Proverbs 15:31,32).

Quest: If you're not big enough to stand
                 criticism, you're too small to be praised.

                              ★

Quip: The sign on the door of opportunity
                 says "Push!"

Quote: "I will be staying here at Ephesus until
                 the holiday of Pentecost, for there is a
                 wide open door for me to preach and
                 teach here. So much is happening, but
                 there are many enemies" (1 Corinthians
                 16:8,9)).

Quest: The trouble with opportunity is that it's
                 always more recognizable going then
                 coming.

Quip: A good laugh is sunshine in a house (Thackeray).

Quote: ''No one had eaten for a long time, but finally Paul called the crew together and said, ''Men, you should have listened to me in the first place and not left Fair Havens—you would have avoided all this injury and loss! But cheer up! Not one of us will lose our lives, even though the ship will go down'' (Acts 27:21,22).

Quest: When a bit of sunshine hits you, after passing of a cloud, when a fit of laughter gets you, and your spine is feelin' proud, don't forget to up and fling it at a soul that's feelin' blue, for the minute that you sling it it's a boomerang to you!

★

Quip: Birds are entangled by their feet and men by their tongues (Fuller).

Quote: ''But no human being can tame the tongue. It is always ready to pour out its deadly poison'' (James 3:8).

Quest: No member needs so great a number of muscles as the tongue; this exceeds all the rest in the number of its movements (Da Vinci).

Quip: The best substitute for experience is
               being 16.

Quote: "Don't let the excitement of being
               young cause you to forget about your
               Creator. Honor him in your youth before
               the evil years come—when you'll no
               longer enjoy living" (Ecclesiastes 12:1).

Quest: Father to teenage son: "Maybe you
               should start to shift for yourself while
               you still know everything."

                            ★

Quip: Life is a rat race—and the rats
               are winning!

Quote: "My life is no longer than my hand! My
               whole lifetime is but a moment to you.
               Proud man! Frail as breath! A shadow!
               And all his busy rushing ends in nothing.
               He heaps up riches for someone else to
               spend. And so, Lord, my only hope is in
               you" (Psalm 39:5-7).

Quest: Look out the window while you're eating
               breakfast. See the bird after the worm,
               the cat ready to pounce on the bird, and
               the dog after the cat. Now you're ready
               to face the business world.

Quip: Don't be afraid to ask dumb questions. They're easier to handle than dumb mistakes.

Quote: "Three days later they finally discovered him. He was in the Temple, sitting among the teachers of Law, discussing deep questions with them and amazing everyone with his understanding and answers" (Luke 2:46,47).

Quest: The greatest of faults, I should say, is to be conscious of none (Carlyle).

★

Quip: Talk is cheap.

Quote: "As you enter the Temple, keep your ears open and your mouth shut! Don't be a fool who doesn't even realize it is sinful to make rash promises to God, for he is in heaven and you are only here on earth, so let your words be few. Just as being too busy gives you nightmares, so being a fool makes you a blabbermouth" (Ecclesiastes 5:1-3).

Quest: Superior people talk about ideas; mediocre people talk about things; little people talk about other people.

Quip: The Bible is criticized most by those
            who read it least.

Quote: "I have thought much about your words,
            and stored them in my heart so that
            they would hold me back from sin"
            (Psalm 119:11).

Quest: It isn't the style of the Bible that makes
            it unpopular with the moderns, but the
            fact that it cramps their style.

                        ★

Quip: A pastor eulogized at a funeral: "The
            shell's here, but the nut's gone."

Quote: "Death came into the world because of
            what one man (Adam) did, and it is
            because of what this other man (Christ)
            has done that now there is the resurrec-
            tion from the dead. Everyone dies
            because all of us are related to Adam,
            being members of his sinful race, and
            wherever there is sin, death results. But
            all who are related to Christ will rise
            again" (1 Corinthians 15:21,22).

Quest: Death is not a period but a comma in
            the story of life.

Quip: You will never stumble if you're on your knees.

Quote: ''Ask, and you will be given what you ask for. Seek, and you will find. Knock, and the door will be opened. For everyone who asks, receives. Anyone who seeks, finds. If only you will knock, the door will open'' (Matthew 7:7,8).

Quest: If God is your Father, please call home.

★

Quip: There are two times to praise the Lord: When you feel like it, and when you don't feel like it.

Quote: ''And I will tell everyone how great and good you are; I will praise you all day long'' (Psalm 35:28).

Quest: The only excuse for not praising the Lord is if you are out of breath: ''Let everything that hath breath praise the Lord'' (Psalm 150:6 KJV).

Quip: The levelheaded person is the one who
                 doesn't get dizzy from doing good turns.

Quote: "And you no doubt know that Jesus of
                 Nazareth was anointed by God with the
                 Holy Spirit and with power, and he went
                 around doing good and healing all who
                 were possessed by demons, for God
                 was with him" (Acts 10:38).

Quest: Do all the good you can, by all the
                 means you can, in all the ways you can,
                 in all the places you can, at all the times
                 you can, to all the people you can, as
                 long as you can.

                              ★

Quip: A father was admonishing his
                 complaining and failing son: "Son, all
                 you need is encouragement and a swift
                 kick in the seat of your can'ts."

Quote: "That night the Lord stood beside Paul
                 and said, "Don't worry, Paul; just as you
                 have told the people about me here in
                 Jerusalem, so you must also in Rome"
                 (Acts 23:11).

Quest: When Thomas Edison's desk was
                 opened years after his death, this card
                 was found among his papers: "When
                 down in the mouth, remember Jonah. He
                 came out all right."

Quip: The egotist says, "Everyone has a right to my opinion."

Quote: "Pride goes before destruction and haughtiness before a fall. Better poor and humble than proud and rich" (Proverbs 16:18,19).

Quest: Be humble or you'll stumble (Moody).

★

Quip: The man who claims to be a self-made man has relieved God of an embarrassing responsibility. He usually is a horrible example of unskilled labor.

Quote: "Pride ends in a fall, while humility brings honor" (Proverbs 29:23).

Quest: Humility is to make a right estimate of one's self (Spurgeon).

Quip: Even a mosquito doesn't get a slap on the back until he starts to work.

Quote: "There is going to come a time of testing at Christ's Judgment Day to see what kind of material each builder has used. Everyone's work will be put through the fire so that all can see whether or not it keeps its value, and what was really accomplished" (1 Corinthians 3:12,13).

Quest: At the working man's house hunger looks in, but dares not enter! Nor will the bailiff or the constable enter; for industry pays debts, but despair increases them (Franklin).

★

Quip: Little Timmy was saying his prayers one night. His mother heard this plea: "And please make Tommy stop throwing things at me. By the way, I've mentioned this before."

Quote: "One day Jesus told his disciples a story to illustrate their need for constant prayer and to show them that they must keep praying until the answer comes" (Luke 18:1).

Quest: Prayer is a powerful thing, for God has bound and tied Himself thereto (Martin Luther).

Quip: Epitaph seen on a stone in a country cemetery: Here lies my darling husband, Walter. May he rest in peace . . .until we meet again.

Quote: "He will give his people strength. He will bless them with peace" (Psalm 29:11).

Quest: Nothing can bring you peace but the triumph of principles (Emerson).

★

Quip: Defeat isn't bitter if you don't swallow it.

Quote: "Who then can ever keep Christ's love from us? When we have trouble or calamity, when we are hunted down or destroyed, is it because he doesn't love us anymore? And if we are hungry, or penniless, or in danger, or threatened with death, has God deserted us? . . .but despite all this, overwhelming victory is ours through Christ who loved us enough to die for us" (Romans 8:35,37).

Quest: There are some defeats more triumphant than victories.

Quip: Everybody is ignorant, only on different subjects (Will Rogers).

Quote: "How thankful I am to Christ Jesus our Lord for choosing me as one of his messengers, and giving me the strength to be faithful to him, even though I used to scoff at the name of Christ. I hunted down his people, harming them in every way I could. But God had mercy on me because I didn't know what I was doing, for I didn't know Christ at the time. Oh, how kind our Lord was, for he showed me how to trust him and become full of love in Jesus Christ" (1 Timothy 1:12-14).

Quest: He who boasts of his own knowledge proclaims his ignorance.

★

Quip: A great many of our troubles are man-maid.

Quote: "For God wants you to be holy and pure, and to keep clear of all sexual sin so that each of you will marry in holiness and honor—not in lustful passion as the heathen do, in their ignorance of God and his ways" (1 Thessalonians 4:3-5).

Quest: One antidote for sexual truancy lies in simply teaching youth the wonder, the miracle, the reverence for the creation of life itself. Life is a divine creation. You don't take chances with creation (Levenson).

Quip: Hint to speaker: If you don't strike oil in ten minutes, quit boring.

Quote: "You brood of snakes! How could evil men like you speak what is good and right? For a man's heart determines his speech. A good man's speech reveals the rich treasures within him. An evil-hearted man is filled with venom, and his speech reveals it" (Matthew 12:34,35).

Quest: What is in the evil well of your heart is bound to come up in the bucket of your speech.

★

Quip: Football coach to high-school team: "Remember, football develops individuality, initiative, and leadership. Now get out there and do exactly what I tell you.

Quote: "Obey your spiritual leaders and be willing to do what they say. For their work is to watch over your souls, and God will judge them on how well they do this" (Hebrews 13:17).

Quest: Initiative is doing the right thing at the right time without being told.

Quip: The quickest way to get back on your
                feet is to get down on your knees.

Quote: "When he calls on me I will answer; I
                will be with him in trouble, and rescue
                him and honor him" (Psalm 91:15).

Quest: He stands best who kneels most; he
                stands strongest who kneels weakest; he
                stands longest who kneels lowest. Bent
                knees make strong backs.

                              ★

Quip: Behold the turtle. He makes progress
                only when he sticks his neck out (James
                Bryant Contant).

Quote: "Then the Lord said to Moses, 'Quit
                praying and get the people moving!
                Forward, march!' " (Exodus 14:15).

Quest: It doesn't matter where you come from
                if you aren't going somewhere.

Quip: He who tunes up in the morning stays in harmony all day.

Quote: "Each morning I will look to you in heaven and lay my requests before you, praying earnestly" (Psalm 5:3).

Quote: Do not have your concert first, then tune your instruments afterwards. Begin the day with the Word of God and prayer, and get first of all in harmony with Him (J. Hudson Taylor).

★

Quip: Don't kill time—it has no resurrection.

Quote: "And remember why he is waiting. He is giving us time to get his message of salvation out to others" (2 Peter 3:15,16).

Quest: Dost thou love life? Then waste not time; for time is the stuff that life is made of (Franklin).

Quip: What the world really needs is more
            young people who will carry to their
            jobs the same enthusiasm for getting
            ahead that they display in traffic.

Quote: "You will find me when you seek me,
            if you look for me in earnest"
            (Jeremiah 29:13).

Quest: Enthusiasm is the best protection in any
            situation. Wholeheartedness is con-
            tagious. Give yourself, if you wish to get
            others (David Seabury).

★

Quip: Church sign: Come in and have your
            faith lifted.

Quote: "Yet faith comes from listening to this
            Good News—the Good News about
            Christ" (Romans 10:17).

Quest: Faith is the pencil of the soul that
            sketches heavenly things.

Quip: Men do not usually reject the Bible because it contradicts itself, but because it contradicts them.

Quote: "The whole Bible was given to us by inspiration from God and is useful to teach us what is true and to make us realize what is wrong in our lives; it straightens us out and helps us do what is right" (2 Timothy 3:16).

Quest: Sin will keep you from the Bible, but the Bible will keep you from sin.

★

Quip: The best way to keep your friends is not to give them away.

Quote: "Wounds from a friend are better than kisses from an enemy" (Proverbs 27:6).

Quest: A friend is a person who goes around saying nice things about you behind your back.

Quip: Worry is like a rocking chair. It gives you
              something to do but doesn't get you
              anyplace.

Quote: "Don't worry about anything; instead,
              pray about everything; tell God your
              needs and don't forget to thank him for
              his answers" (Philippians 4:6).

Quest: Worry is the interest you pay when you
              borrow trouble.

★

Quip: You can never make your dreams come
              true by oversleeping.

Quote: "After I have poured out my rains again,
              I will pour out my Spirit upon all of you!
              Your sons and daughters will prophesy;
              your old men will dream dreams, and
              your young men see visions" (Joel 2:28).

Quest: A man gazing at the stars is at the
              mercy of the puddles on the road
              (Alexander Smith).

Quip: Many a man has battled his way to the top and bottled his way to the bottom.

Quote: "Wine gives false courage; hard liquor leads to brawls; what fools men are to let it master them, making them reel drunkenly down the street!"
(Proverbs 20:1).

Quest: There is a devil in every berry of the grape (Koran).

★

Quip: You cannot kill time without injuring eternity.

Quote: "Teach us to number our days and recognize how few they are; help us to spend them as we should"
(Psalm 90:12).

Quest: Counting time is not as important as making time count (James J. Walker).

Quip: Your brain is no stronger than its
                   weakest think.

Quote: ''A good man's mind is filled with honest
                   thoughts; an evil man's mind is crammed
                   with lies'' (Proverbs 12:5).

Quest: You are not responsible for the thoughts
                   that pass your door. You are responsible
                   for those you admit and entertain.

                                   ★

Quip: Those who stretch the truth usually find
                   that it snaps back.

Quote: ''A man who is caught lying to his
                   neighbor and says, 'I was just fooling,' is
                   like a madman throwing around
                   firebrands, arrows and death!''
                   (Proverbs 26:18,19).

Quest: If we could see ourselves as others see
                   us, we wouldn't even have the nerve
                   to ''be us.''

Quip: Seven days without worship makes one weak.

Quote: "Yes, ascribe to the Lord the glory due his name! Bring an offering and come before him; Worship the Lord when clothed with holiness!" (1 Chronicles 16:29).

Quest: The wonderous architect of the human body points unmistakably to the wise Creator who has destined you for eternity. Worship Him. He is worthy.

★

Quip: The world needs more warm hearts and fewer hot heads.

Quote: "There are 'friends' who pretend to be friends, but there is a friend who sticks closer than a brother" (Proverbs 18:24).

Quest: Real friends are those who, when you've made a fool of yourself, don't feel that you've done a permanent job.

Quip: Flattery is soft soap, and soap is 90
             percent lye. A flatterer is a man who
             soft-soaps a woman until she can't see
             for the suds.

Quote: "Flattery is a trap; evil men are caught
             in it, but good men stay away and sing
             for joy" (Proverbs 29:5,6).

Quest: Flattery is a sort of bad money, to which
             your vanity gives currency.

★

Quip: A lie will go around the world while the
             truth is getting its boots on (Dwight L.
             Moody).

Quote: "Then watch your tongue! Keep your
             lips from lying" (Psalm 34:13).

Quest: A lie can be dressed up to look like the
             truth, but the dress will wear out.

Quip: To avoid a hot argument, keep a cool head.

Quote: "Yanking a dog's ear is no more foolish than interfering in an argument that isn't any of your business" (Proverbs 26:17).

Quest: A sound argument must have more than sound to it. "A man convinced against his will is of the same opinion still" (Butler).

★

Quip: People who gossip usually end up in their own mouth traps.

Quote: "An evil man sows strife; gossip separates the best of friends" (Proverbs 16:28).

Quest: There is so much good in the worst of us, and so much bad in the best of us, that it hardly behooves any of us to talk about the rest of us.

Quip: The prevention of crime begins in the
                 high chair, not the electric chair.

Quote: ''If you refuse to discipline your son, it
                 proves you don't love him; for if you
                 love him you will be prompt to punish
                 him'' (Proverbs 13:24).

Quest: The behavior of some children suggests
                 that their parents embarked on the sea
                 of matrimony without a paddle.

                              ★

Quip: Make long-range plans as if you were
                 going to live forever, and live today as if
                 it were your last day on earth.

Quote: ''We can make our plans, but the final
                 outcome is in God's hands'' (Proverbs
                 16:1).

Quest: One of the greatest things about life is
                 not so much where we stand as in what
                 direction we are going.

Quip: What you are is God's gift to you. What you make of yourself is your gift to God.

Quote: "And so, dear brothers, I plead with you to give your bodies to God. Let them be a living sacrifice, holy—the kind he can accept. When you think of what he has done for you, is this too much to ask? Don't copy the behavior and customs of this world, but be a new and different person with a fresh newness in all you do and think. Then you will learn from your own experience how his ways will really satisfy you" (Romans 12:1,2).

Quest: Give yourself to God. He can do more with you than you can.

★

Quip: Cooperation will solve many problems. Even freckles would make a nice coat of tan if they'd only get together!

Quote: "How wonderful it is, how pleasant, when brothers live in harmony" (Psalm 133:1).

Quest: Who passed the ball to you when *you* scored?

Quip: It's not so much the size of the dog in
              the fight that counts, but the size of the
              fight in the dog.

Quote: "Put on all of God's armor so that you
              will be able to stand safe against all
              strategies and tricks of Satan. For we are
              not fighting against people made of flesh
              and blood, but against persons without
              bodies—the evil rulers of the unseen
              world, those mighty satanic beings and
              great evil princes of darkness who rule
              this world; and against the huge
              numbers of wicked spirits in the spirit
              world" (Ephesians 6:11,12).

Quest: Resisting adversity causes some men to
              break, others to break records.

                              ★

Quip: Success comes in cans; failure comes in
              can'ts (Fred Seeley).

Quote: "For I can do everything God asks me to
              with the help of Christ who gives me the
              strength and power" (Philippians 4:13).

Quest: Success is getting up one more time
              than falling down.

Quip: Sign on a Pentagon executive's desk: "This job is so secret I don't know what I'm doing.

Quote: "Work hard so God can say to you, 'Well done.' Be a good workman, one who does not need to be ashamed when God examines your work. Know what his Word says and means" (2 Timothy 2:15).

Quest: Stupidity is forever; ignorance can be fixed.

★

Quip: Your conscience makes you tell your wife before someone else does.

Quote: "Cling tightly to your faith in Christ and always keep your conscience clear, doing what you know is right. For some people have disobeyed their consciences and have deliberately done what they knew was wrong. It isn't surprising that soon they lost their faith in Christ after defying God like that" (1 Timothy 1:19).

Quest: Conscience is a playback of the still, small voice that told you not to do it in the first place.

Quip: We wouldn't necessarily call him a liar.
               Let's just say he lives on the wrong side
               of the facts.

Quote: "What a shame—yes, how stupid!—to
               decide before knowing the facts! . . .Any
               story sounds true until someone tells the
               other side and sets the record straight"
               (Proverbs 18:13,17).

Quest: Facts do not cease to exist because they
               are ignored.

                            ★

Quip: The reason ideas die quickly in some
               people's heads is because they can't
               stand solitary confinement.

Quote: "Do not despise this small beginning, for
               the eyes of the Lord rejoice to see the
               work begin" (Zechariah 4:10).

Quest: A new idea is delicate. It can be killed
               by a sneer or a yawn, stabbed to death
               by a quip, or worried to death by a
               frown.

Quip: When it comes to giving, some people stop at nothing.

Quote: "Everyone must make up his own mind as to how much he should give. Don't force anyone to give more than he really wants to, for cheerful givers are the ones God prizes" (2 Corinthians 9:7).

Quest: The exchange of Christmas gifts ought to be reciprocal rather than retaliatory.

★

Quip: "Whines" are the products of sour grapes.

Quote: "Don't just think about your own affairs, but be interested in others, too, and in what they are doing. Your attitude should be the kind that was shown us by Jesus Christ" (Philippians 2:4,5).

Quest: A man who sits in a swamp all day waiting to shoot a duck but gripes if his wife has dinner ten minutes late is a miserable soul.

Quip: One fellow said, "I may have had
                   relatives who hung from trees, but it was
                   by their necks, not their tails."

Quote: "That man is a fool who says to himself,
                   'There is no God!'" (Psalm 14:1).

Quest: There are no atheists in foxholes.

★

Quip: Life is a continuous process of getting
                   used to things we hadn't expected.

Quote: "Stay away from love of money; be
                   satisfied with what you have. For God
                   has said, 'I will never, never fail you or
                   forsake you.' That is why we can say
                   without any doubt or fear, 'The Lord is
                   my Helper and I am not afraid of
                   anything that mere man can do to me' "
                   (Hebrews 13:5,6).

Quest: Nothing in life is as easy as it looks.
                   Everything takes longer than you expect,
                   and if anything can go wrong, it will, at
                   the worst possible moment. There are
                   no simple solutions—only intelligent
                   ones.

Quip: The tongue is only three inches long, yet it can kill a man six feet tall.

Quote: "Some people like to make cutting remarks, but the words of the wise soothe and heal" (Proverbs 12:18).

Quest: The tongue can be a blessing, and the tongue can be a curse; say, how are you using yours—for better or for worse?

★

Quip: The only fellow whose troubles are all behind him is a school-bus driver.

Quote: "I want you to trust me in your times of trouble, so I can rescue you, and you can give me glory" (Psalm 50:15).

Quest: The best way for you to meet trouble is to face it.

Quip: The only people who listen to both sides of the argument are the neighbors.

Quote: "There's no use arguing with a fool. He only rages and scoffs, and tempers flare" (Proverbs 29:9).

Quest: An argument occurs when two people try to get the last word in first.

★

Quip: The person who wakes up and finds himself a success hasn't been asleep.

Quote: "If you love sleep, you will end in poverty. Stay awake, work hard, and there will be plenty to eat!" (Proverbs 20:13).

Quest: On the plains lie the bleaching bones of millions who, on the verge of success, sat down to rest; while resting, they died.

Quip: Since you have two ears and one mouth, you should hear twice as much as you speak.

Quote: "Every young man who listens to me and obeys my instructions will be given wisdom and good sense" (Proverbs 2:1).

Quest: A man never listened himself out of a job (Calvin Coolidge).

★

Quip: Prayer is the stop that keeps you going.

Quote: "Ask, and you will be given what you ask for. Seek, and you will find. Knock, and the door will be opened" (Matthew 7:7).

Quest: Sign on church marquee: Our church is prayer-conditioned.

Quip: The best place to find a helping hand is
                   at the end of your own arm.

Quote: ''Whatever you do, do well, for in death,
                   where you are going, there is no work-
                   ing or planning, or knowing, or
                   understanding'' (Ecclesiastes 9:10).

Quest: You can't help someone else uphill
                   without getting closer to the top
                   yourself.

                              ★

Quip: The hypocrite believes that life is what
                   you fake it.

Quote: ''Hypocrite! First get rid of the board.
                   Then you can see to help your
                   brother . . .Ask, and you will be given
                   what you ask for. Seek, and you will
                   find. Knock, and the door will be
                   opened'' (Matthew 7:5, 7).

Quest: Clean your fingers well before you point
                   at another's faults (Benjamin Franklin).

Quip: If you stop at third base to congratulate yourself, you'll never score a home run.

Quote: "I have fought a good fight, I have finished my course, I have kept the faith" (2 Timothy 4:7 KJV).

Quest: A diamond is a piece of coal that stuck to its job.

★

Quip: The brain is no stronger than its weakest think.

Quote: "And now, brothers, as I close this letter let me say this one more thing: Fix your thoughts on what is true and good and right. Think about things that are pure and lovely, and dwell on the fine, good things in others. Think about all you can praise God for and be glad about" (Philippians 4:8).

Quest: Be careful of your thoughts—they may break into words at any time.

Quip: A stingy guy who never picks up the
              dinner check has an impediment in his
              reach.

Quote: "And I was a constant example to you
              in helping the poor; for I remembered
              the words of the Lord Jesus, 'It is more
              blessed to give than to receive' "
              (Acts 20:35).

Quest: The manner of giving shows the
              character of the giver more than the gift
              itself (Lavater).

                          ★

Quip: Money is a good servant but a
              dangerous master.

Quote: "For the love of money is the first step
              toward all kinds of sin. Some people
              have even turned away from God
              because of their love for it, and as a
              result have pierced themselves with
              many sorrows" (1 Timothy 6:10).

Quest: If you make money your god, it will
              plague you like the devil (Fielding).

Quip: He who fiddles around seldom gets to lead the orchestra.

Quote: "Don't be fools; be wise: make the most of every opportunity you have for doing good" (Ephesians 5:16).

Quest: Strange, isn't it? Everybody wants to harvest, but few want to plow.

★

Quip: Let us endeavor to so live that, when we come to die, even the undertaker will be sorry (Mark Twain).

Quote: "Don't hide your light! Let it shine for all; let your good deeds glow for all to see, so that they will praise your heavenly Father (Matthew 5:15,16).

Quest: Lives of great men all remind us that we can make our lives sublime, and when departing leave behind us footprints in the sands of time (Longfellow).

Quip: Feed your faith and your doubts will
                 starve to death.

Quote: "You can never please God without
                 faith, without depending on him. Anyone
                 who wants to come to God must believe
                 that there is a God and that he rewards
                 those who sincerely look for him"
                 (Hebrews 11:6).

Quest: Keep faith as a constant companion.
                 When Fear knocks at your door, send
                 Faith to answer it (Ralph Beebe).

★

Quip: Many a wife manages her husband by
                 simply using a little sigh-chology.

Quote: "That is how husbands should treat their
                 wives, loving them as parts of
                 themselves. For since a man and his wife
                 are now one, a man is really doing
                 himself a favor and loving himself when
                 he loves his wife." (Ephesians 5:28).

Quest: "Help your wife," advised a home-
                 economics lecturer. "When she washes
                 the dishes, wash the dishes with her;
                 when she mops the floor, mop the floor
                 with her."

Quip: The so-called weaker sex is the stronger
             sex because of the weakness of the
             stronger sex for the weaker sex.

Quote: "So again I say, a man must love his
             wife as a part of himself; and the wife
             must see to it that she deeply respects
             her husband—obeying, praising and
             honoring him" (Ephesians 5:33).

Quest: He is a fool who thinks by force or skill
             to turn the current of a woman's will
             (Tom Moore).

★

Quip: Critics are people who go places and
             boo things.

Quote: "Don't criticize and speak evil about
             each other, dear brothers. If you do, you
             will be fighting against God's law of
             loving one another, declaring it is wrong.
             But your job is not to decide whether
             this law is right or wrong, but to obey
             it" (James 4:11).

Quest: Have you ever noticed that most
             knocking is done by folks who don't
             know how to ring the bell?

Quip: He who throws dirt loses ground.

Quote: Only he who made the law can rightly
                judge among us. He alone decides to
                save us or destroy. So what right do you
                have to judge or criticize others?"
                (James 4:12).

Quest: Bernard Baruch once reminded us that
                two things are hard on the heart—
                running up stairs and running down
                people.

                              ★

Quip: The best way to save face is to keep the
                lower part shut.

Quote: "Keep your mouth closed and you'll stay
                out of trouble" (Proverbs 21:23).

Quest: When you are in deep water, be sure to
                keep your mouth shut.

Quip: He who asks a question may be a fool for five minutes, but he who never asks a question remains a fool forever.

Quote: "Determination to be wise is the first step toward becoming wise! And with your wisdom, develop common sense and good judgment" (Proverbs 4:7).

Quest: Four and twenty are the most desirable ages; at four you know all the questions; at twenty you know all the answers.

★

Quip: A small boy's ambition: to grow up and be a farmer so he can get paid for not growing spinach.

Quote: "This should be your ambition: to live a quiet life, minding your own business and doing your own work, just as we told you before" (1 Thessalonians 4:11).

Quest: Talking with Mark Twain, the humorist, a man stated that his greatest wish and ambition was to visit Mount Sinai and there see the place where God gave Moses the Ten Commandments. Mark Twain responded by saying, "Why don't you just stay home and keep the Ten Commandments?"

Quip: If you lie down with the dogs, you'll get
                up with the fleas.

Quote: "Be with wise men and become wise. Be
                with evil men and become evil"
                (Proverbs 13:20).

Quest: Keep company with good men, and
                good men you'll imitate.

★

Quip: The loser says, "The worst is just around
                the corner." The winner says, "The best
                is yet to come."

Quote: "Always be full of joy in the Lord; I say
                it again, rejoice! Let everyone see that
                you are unselfish and considerate in all
                you do. Remember that the Lord is
                coming soon. Don't worry about
                anything; instead, pray about everything;
                tell God your needs and don't forget
                to thank him for his answers"
                (Philippians 4:4-6).

Quest: Disregard your complaints and discover
                your gratitude. Release your trouble and
                restate your blessings.

Quip: He did nothing in particular, and did it very well (Gilbert).

Quote: ''I walked by the field of a certain lazy fellow and saw that it was overgrown with thorns, and covered with weeds; and its walls were broken down. Then, as I looked, I learned this lesson: 'A little extra sleep, a little more slumber, a little folding of the hands to rest' means that poverty will break in upon you suddenly like a robber, and violently like a bandit'' (Proverbs 24:30-34).

Quest: Idleness is a holiday of fools (Chesterfield).

★

Quip: The most fortunate thing about small boys is that they're washable.

Quote: ''How can a young man stay pure? By reading your Word and following its rules'' (Psalm 119:9).

Quest: Live as long as you may, the first twenty years are the longest half of your life (Southey).

Quip: Some people can stay longer in an hour than others can in a week (Howells).

Quote: "Don't talk so much. You keep putting your foot in your mouth. Be sensible and turn off the flow! When a good man speaks, he is worth listening to, but the words of fools are a dime a dozen" (Proverbs 10:19,20).

Quest: The cure for boredom is curiosity. There is no cure for curiosity (Parr).

★

Quip: Your life is fragile—handle with prayer.

Quote: "How do you know what is going to happen tomorrow? For the length of your lives is as uncertain as the morning fog—now you see it; soon it is gone. What you ought to say is, 'If the Lord wants us to, we shall live and do this or that' " (James 4:14,15).

Quest: I expect to pass through this life but once. Any good therefore that I can do, or any kindness that I can show to any fellow creature, let me do it now. Let me not defer it, for I shall not pass this way again.

Quip: Do not squander time, for that is the stuff life is made of (Benjamin Franklin).

Quote: "So be careful how you act; these are difficult days. Don't be fools; be wise: make the most of every opportunity you have for doing good" (Ephesians 5:15, 16).

Quest: If you kill time, you'll bury opportunities.

★

Quip: The trouble with life is that by the time a fellow gets to be an old hand at the game, he starts losing his grip (Peace).

Quote: "Listen to me, all Israel who are left; I have created you and cared for you since you were born. I will be your God through all your lifetime, yes, even when your hair is white with age. I made you and I will care for you. I will carry you along and be your Savior" (Isaiah 46:3,4).

Quest: There are three things that grow more precious with age: old wool to burn, old books to read, and old friends to enjoy.

Quip: Do not mistake activity for achievement.

Quote: "Listen to me! You can pray for
                   everything, and *if you believe, you have it*; it's
                   yours!" (Mark 11:24).

Quest: If your mind can conceive it, and your
                   heart can believe it, then you can
                   achieve it.

★

Quip: He that is overcautious will accomplish
                   little (Schiller).

Quote: "Whatever you do, do well, for in death,
                   where you are going, there is no
                   working or planning, or knowing, or
                   understanding" (Ecclesiastes 9:10).

Quest: He started to sing as he tackled the
                   thing that couldn't be done, and he did
                   it (Guest).

Quip: Experience is a strenuous teacher. No graduates, no degrees, some survivors.

Quote: "The steps of good men are directed by the Lord. He delights in each step they take. If they fall it isn't fatal, for the Lord holds them with his hand. I have been young and now I am old. And in all my years I have never seen the Lord forsake a man who loves him; nor have I seen the children of the godly go hungry" (Psalm 37:23-25)..

Quest: Experience should be a guidepost and not a hitching post.

★

Quip: A pat on the back develops character, if it is administered young enough, often enough, and low enough.

Quote: "Don't fail to corrrect your children; discipline won't hurt them! They won't die if you use a stick on them! Punishment will keep them out of hell" (Proverbs 23:13,14).

Quest: The sturdiest tree is not found in the shelter of the forest, but high upon some rocky crag, where its daily battle with the elements shapes it into a thing of beauty. So it is with you.

Quip: Wife to husband: "Seven o'clock, dear.
Time to get up and start worrying."

Quote: "Stop your anger! Turn off your wrath.
Don't fret and worry—it only leads to
harm. For the wicked shall be destroyed,
but those who trust the Lord shall be
given every blessing" (Psalm 37:8,9).

Quest: One of the worst things you can possibly
do is to worry and think about what you
could have done.

★

Quip: There's one thing about getting fired;
it helps you make up your mind
(C.M. Ward).

Quote: "I call heaven and earth to witness
against you that today I have set before
you life or death, blessing or curse. Oh,
that you would choose life; that you and
your children might live! Choose to love
the Lord your God and to obey him and
to cling to him, for he is your life and
the length of your days. You will then be
able to live safely in the land the Lord
promised your ancestors, Abraham,
Isaac, and Jacob" (Deuteronomy
30:19,20).

Quest: Your decisions must be based on *what* is
right, not on *who* is right. History is made
when you make a decision.

Quip: Forty is the old age of youth; fifty is the
               youth of old age.

Quote: "After I have poured out my rains again,
               I will pour out my Spirit upon all of you!
               Your sons and daughters will prophesy;
               your old men will dream dreams, and
               your young men see visions" (Joel 2:28).

Quest: Of course life doesn't begin at 40 if you
               went like 60 when you were 20.

★

Quip: A rabbit is not supposed to climb trees,
               but sometimes he must.

Quote: "Be strong and brave, for you will be a
               successful leader of my people; and they
               shall conquer all the land I promised to
               their ancestors. You need only to be
               strong and courageous and to obey to
               the letter every law Moses gives you, for
               if you are careful to obey every one of
               them you will be successful in everything
               you do" (Joshua 1:6,7).

Quest: Necessity makes even the timid brave
               (Sallust).

Quip: An efficiency expert is a man who walks
                 in his sleep so he can get his rest and
                 exercise at the same time.

Quote: "To win the contest you must deny
                 yourselves many things that would keep
                 you from doing your best. An athlete
                 goes to all this trouble just to win a blue
                 ribbon or a silver cup, but we do it for a
                 heavenly reward that never disappears.
                 So I run straight to the goal with
                 purpose in every step. I fight to win. I'm
                 not just shadow-boxing or playing
                 around" (1 Corinthians 9:25,26).

Quest: The best carpenter makes the fewest
                 chips.

★

Quip: Faith is telling a mountain to move and
                 being shocked only if it doesn't.

Quote: "For if you had faith even as small as a
                 tiny mustard seed you could say to this
                 mountain, 'Move!' and it would go far
                 away. Nothing would be impossible"
                 (Matthew 17:20).

Quest: Faith hears the inaudible, sees the
                 invisible, believes the incredible, and
                 receives the impossible.

Quip: Education covers a lot of ground, but it doesn't cultivate it.

Quote: "The man who knows right from wrong and has good judgment and common sense is happier than the man who is immensely rich! For such wisdom is far more valuable than precious jewels. Nothing else compares with it" (Proverbs 3:13-15).

Quest: There are three great questions which in life we have to answer over and over again: Is it right or wrong? It is true or false? Is it beautiful or ugly? Our education ought to help us answer these questions (Lubbock).

★

Quip: Nobody is completely worthless. If nothing else, a person can serve as a horrible example.

Quote: "Keep putting into practice all you learned from me and saw me doing, and the God of peace will be with you" (Philippians 4:9).

Quest: Lives of great men all remind us that we can make our lives sublime, and, when departing, leave behind us footprints on the sands of time (Longfellow).

Quip: The best way to get rid of your duties is to discharge them.

Quote: ''When a servant comes in from plowing or taking care of sheep, he doesn't just sit down and eat, but first prepares his master's meal and serves him his supper before he eats his own. And he is not even thanked, for he is merely doing what he is supposed to do. Just so, if you merely obey me, you should not consider yourselves worthy of praise. For you have simply done your duty!'' (Luke 17:7-10).

Quest: Duty without enthusiasm becomes laborious; duty with enthusiasm becomes glorious (Ward).

★

Quip: A war movie being shown on French television showed an American GI pointing to the horizon. ''Tanks!'' he said to another GI, and the caption read ''Merci!''

Quote: ''No matter what happens, always be thankful, for this is God's will for you who belong to Christ Jesus (1 Thessalonians 5:18).

Quest: If you can't be thankful for what you receive, be thankful for what you escape.

Quip: In God we trust. All others pay cash.

Quote: ''The very day I call for help, the tide of battle turns. My enemies flee! This one thing I know: God is for me! I am trusting God—oh, praise his promises! I am not afraid of anything mere man can do to me! Yes, praise his promises!'' (Psalm 56:9-11).

Quest: Trust in God, and keep your powder dry (Cromwell).

★

Quip: Never trouble trouble until trouble troubles you.

Quote: ''And so I would say to you who are suffering, God will give you rest along with us when the Lord Jesus appears suddenly from heaven in flaming fire with his mighty angels, bringing judgment on those who do not wish to know God, and who refuse to accept his plan to save them through our Lord Jesus Christ (2 Thessalonians 1:7,8).

Quest: The true way to soften your troubles is to help others in theirs.

Quip: Before you complain about the darkness
              of the tunnel, remember that it is a
              shortcut through the mountains.

Quote: "Your words are a flashlight to light the
              path ahead of me, and keep me from
              stumbling" (Psalm 119:105).

Quest: You will discover that it is always
              darkest just before the dawn.

                            ★

Quip: To take care to bed is to sleep with a
              pack on your back.

Quote: "Let him have all your worries and
              cares, for he is always thinking about
              you and watching everything that
              concerns you" (1 Peter 5:7).

Quest: If a care is too small for you to turn into
              a prayer, it is too small for you to turn
              into a burden.

Quip: Cheerfulness will open a door when other keys fail.

Quote: ''A cheerful heart does good like medicine, but a broken spirit makes one sick'' (Proverbs 17:22).

Quest: Sing and you'll frighten away your ills.

★

Quip: Too many people who say ''Our Father'' on Sunday spend the rest of the week acting like orphans.

Quote: ''They worshiped together regularly at the Temple each day, met in small groups in homes for Communion, and shared their meals with great joy and thankfulness, praising God'' (Acts 2:46).

Quest: Church membership does not make you a Christian any more than owning a piano makes you a musician.

Quip: There are some people so addicted to
                 exaggeration that they can't tell the truth
                 without lying.

Quote: "Get the facts at any price, and hold on
                 tight to all the good sense you can get"
                 (Proverbs 23:23).

Quest: A diplomatic teacher sent this note
                 home to all parents: "If you promise not
                 to believe everything your child says
                 happens at school, I'll promise not to
                 believe everything he says happens at
                 home."

★

Quip: Our idea of a contented man is the one
                 who enjoys the scenery along the
                 detour.

Quote: "Stay away from the love of money; be
                 satisfied with what you have. For God
                 has said, 'I will never, never fail you nor
                 forsake you' " (Hebrews 13:5).

Quest: The secret of contentment is knowing
                 how to enjoy what you have, and to be
                 able to lose all desire for things beyond
                 your reach (Yutang).

Quip: The person who says the art of conversation is dead has never stood outside a phone booth in the rain waiting for someone to finish talking.

Quote: "If anyone can control his tongue, it proves that he has perfect control over himself in every other way" (James 3:2).

Quest: A single conversation across the table with a wise man is worth a month's study of books.

★

Quip: A sharp nose is said to indicate curiosity, while a flattened one is the result of trying to satisfy it.

Quote: "When reports of Jesus' miracles reached Herod, the governor, he was worried and puzzled, for some were saying, 'This is John the Baptist come back to life again'; and others, 'It is Elijah or some other ancient prophet risen from the dead.' Those rumors were circulating all over the land. 'I beheaded John,' Herod said, 'so who is this man about whom I hear such strange stories?' And he tried to see him" (Luke 9:7-9).

Quest: The overcurious are not always overwise.

Quip: The wildest colts make the best horses (Plutarch).

Quote: "My son, never forget the things I've taught you. If you want a long and satisfying life, closely follow my instructions. Never forget to be truthful and kind. Hold these virtues tightly. Write them deep within your heart. If you want favor with both God and man, and a reputation for good judgment and common sense, then trust the Lord completely; don't ever trust yourself" (Proverbs 3:1-5).

Quest: One teenager to another: "The trouble with my father is that he remembers what it's like to be young."

★

Quip: Prayer flies where the eagle never flew.

Quote: "But they that wait upon the Lord shall renew their strength. They shall mount up with wings like eagles; they shall run and not be weary; they shall walk and not faint" (Isaiah 40:31).

Quest: If you will work *for* God, form a committee. If you will work *with* God, form a prayer group.

Quip: An umpire's favorite dessert is rhubarb pie.

Quote: "Yes, each of us will give an account of himself to God. So don't criticize each other any more. Try instead to live in such a way that you will never make your brother stumble by letting him see you doing something he thinks is wrong" (Romans 14:12,13).

Quest: Whether we want to admit it or not, most of us are umpires at heart; we like to call balls and strikes on other people.

★

Quip: New automobiles come equipped with a right-turn and left-turn signal. What we need is one more to indicate "undecided."

Quote: "But when you ask him, be sure that you really expect him to tell you, for a doubtful mind will be as unsettled as a wave of the sea that is driven and tossed by the wind; and every decision you then make will be uncertain, as you turn first this way, and then that. If you don't ask with faith, don't expect the Lord to give you any solid answer" (James 1:6-8).

Quest: You must decide on what you will not do, and then you will be able to act with vigor in what you ought to do.

Quip: If silence is golden, not many people
              can be arrested for hoarding.

Quote: "For the Lord God, the Holy One of
              Israel, says: Only in returning to me and
              waiting for me will you be saved; in
              quietness and confidence in your
              strength" (Isaiah 30:15).

Quest: Conversation enriches the understand-
              ing, but solitude is the school of genius
              (Gibbon).

                            ★

Quip: It is better to understand little than to
              misunderstand a lot (France).

Quote: "Your laws are wonderful; no wonder I
              obey them. As your plan unfolds, even
              the simple can understand it. No wonder
              I wait expectantly for each of your
              commands" (Psalm 119:129-131).

Quest: Instead of putting others in their place,
              try putting yourself in their place.

Quip: A child defined impatience as "waiting in a hurry."

Quote: "Be glad for all God is planning for you. Be patient in trouble, and prayerful always" (Romans 12:12).

Quest: All things come round to him who will but wait (Longfellow).

★

Quip: "Impossible" is a word only to be found in the dictionary of fools (Napoleon).

Quote: "Jesus looked at them intently, then said, 'Without God, it is utterly impossible. But with God everything is possible'" (Mark 10:27).

Quest: You do not test the resources of God until you attempt the impossible (Meyer).

Quip: The lazier a man is the more he plans to do tomorrow.

Quote: "Take a lesson from the ants, you lazy fellow. Learn from their ways and be wise! For though they have no king to make them work, yet they labor hard all summer, gathering food for the winter. But you—all you do is sleep. When will you wake up? 'Let me sleep a little longer!' Sure, just a little more! And as you sleep, poverty creeps upon you like a robber and destroys you; want attacks you in full armor" (Proverbs 6:6-11).

Quest: Six-thirty is my time to rise, but I'm seldom bright of eye; part of me says "Look alive!" and the other part asks "Why?"

★

Quip: The diamond cannot be polished without friction, nor man perfected without trials.

Quote: "Dear friends, don't be bewildered or surprised when you go through the fiery trials ahead, for this is no strange, unusual thing that is going to happen to you. Instead, be really glad—because these trials will make you partners with Christ in his suffering, and afterwards you will have the wonderful joy of sharing his glory in that coming day when it will be displayed" (1 Peter 4:12,13).

Quest: There are no crown-wearers in heaven who were not cross-bearers here below (Spurgeon).

Quip: Tears are often the telescope through which men see far into heaven.

Quote: "His anger lasts for a moment; his favor lasts for life! Weeping may go on all night, but in the morning there is joy" (Psalm 30:5).

Quest: Never a tear that bedims the eye that time and patience will not dry (Harte).

★

Quip: The most important evidence of tolerance is a golden wedding anniversary.

Quote: "We are no longer Jews or Greeks or slaves or free men or merely men or women, but we are all the same—we are Christians; we are one in Christ Jesus" (Galatians 3:28).

Quest: I do not agree with a word you say, but I will defend to the death your right to say it (Voltaire).

Quip: He who expects nothing shall never be disappointed.

Quote: "You can never please God without faith, without depending on him. Anyone who wants to come to God must believe that there is a God and that he rewards those who sincerely look for him" (Hebrews 11:6).

Quest: All I have seen teaches me to trust the Creator for all I have not seen (Emerson).

★

Quip: He who talks without thinking runs more risks than he who thinks without talking.

Quote: "Keep a close watch on all you do and think. Stay true to what is right and God will bless you and use you to help others (1 Timothy 4:16).

Quest: Some people talk to express their thoughts; some talk to conceal their thoughts; but most just talk to keep from thinking.

Quip: The ability to speak several languages is valuable, but the art of keeping silent in one is precious.

Quote: "A wise man holds his tongue. Only a fool blurts out everything he knows; that only leads to sorrow and trouble" (Proverbs 10:14).

Quest: The things you say and do today, in memory's book, you'll keep, and when you're old and read them, will you laugh or will you weep?

★

Quip: The best way out of difficulties is through them.

Quote: "Dear brothers, is your life full of difficulties and temptations? Then be happy, for when the way is rough, your patience has a chance to grow. So let it grow, and don't try to squirm out of your problems. For when your patience is finally in full bloom, then you will be ready for anything, strong in character, full and complete" (James 1:2-4).

Quest: The three most difficult things are: to keep a secret, to forget an injury, and to make good use of leisure (Chilo).

Quip: The toughest form of mountain climbing is getting out of a rut.

Quote: "You are living a brand new kind of life that is continually learning more and more of what is right, and trying constantly to be more and more like Christ who created this new life within you. In this new life one's nationality or race or education or social position is unimportant; such things mean nothing. Whether a person has Christ is what matters, and he is equally available to all" (Colossians 3:10,11).

Quest: If you are caught in the ruts of worldliness and wrong living, you need to plant your life's roots in new soil, so you can enjoy the rights of Christian living.

★

Quip: The big rewards come to those who travel the second undemanded mile.

Quote: "If you are slapped on one cheek, turn the other too. If you are ordered to court, and your shirt is taken from you, give your coat too. If the military demand that you carry their gear for a mile, carry it two" (Matthew 5:39-41).

Quest: To receive a reward is good; to deserve it is much better.

Quip: Character is what you really are;
reputation is only what others believe
you to be.

Quote: "A good reputation is more valuable
than the most expensive perfume"
(Ecclesiastes 7:1).

Quest: Your reputation is made by searching
for things that can't be done—and doing
them.

★

Quip: If you think that one person can't make
a difference in the world, consider what
one cigar can do in a crowded
restaurant.

Quote: "No one will be able to oppose you as
long as you live, for I will be with you
just as I was with Moses; I will not
abandon you or fail to help you. Be
strong and brave, for you will be a
successful leader of my people; and they
shall conquer all the land I promised to
their ancestors" (Joshua 1:5,6).

Quest: You have a place to fill in the world, one
no one else can fill. You are important
in God's plan whether you want to
believe it or not.

Quip: Nothing makes an office worker more
              punctual than 5 P.M.

Quote: "So be prepared, for you don't know
              what day your Lord is coming. Just as a
              man can prevent trouble from thieves by
              keeping watch for them, so you can
              avoid trouble by always being ready for
              my unannounced return" (Matthew
              24:42-44).

Quest: He was a man honored and respected
              for three things: promptness,
              punctuality, and not being late.

                          ★

Quip: God didn't promise an easy voyage, but
              a safe arrival.

Quote: "And we know that all that happens to
              us is working for our good if we love
              God and are fitting into his plans"
              (Romans 8:28).

Quest: It is when you give up battling the
              storms in your own ability and turn to
              Him that you find relief and rest.

Quip:　　Prayer: Even the feeblest knock is heard on heaven's door.

Quote:　　"Ask, and you will be given what you ask for. Seek, and you will find. Knock, and the door will be opened" (Matthew 7:7).

Quest:　　Pray in faith. If a friend gave you a check, would you wait until you cashed it to thank him?

★

Quip:　　Political campaign: a matter of mud, threats, and smears.

Quote:　　"If a godly man compromises with the wicked, it is like polluting a fountain or muddying a spring" (Proverbs 25:26). "A double-minded man is unstable in all his ways" (James 1:8 KJV).

Quest:　　Probably the reason why a politician stands on his record is to keep voters from examining it.

Quip: It's the little things that bother us and put us on the rack; you can sit upon a mountain but you can't sit on a tack!

Quote: "The little foxes are ruining the vineyards. Catch them, for the grapes are all in blossom" (Song of Solomon 2:15).

Quest: Not what you have, but what you see; not what you see, but what you choose, not what seems fair, but what is true; not what you dream, but what you do; not what you take, but what you give; not as you pray, but as you live. These are the things that mar or bless the sum of human happiness.

★

Quip: There are two types of people in the world: those who come into the room and say, "Well, here I am!" and those who come and say, "Ah, there you are!"

Quote: "True humility and respect for the Lord lead a man to riches, honor and long life" (Proverbs 22:4).

Quest: Humility is a strange thing: The moment you think you have it, you have lost it.

Quip: If you have teenagers in your house, you'll find it difficult to understand how farmers could possibly grow a surplus of food.

Quote: "And now a word to you parents. Don't keep on scolding and nagging your children, making them angry and resentful. Rather, bring them up with the loving discipline the Lord himself approves, with suggestions and godly advice" (Ephesians 6:4).

Quest: Note on church bulletin board: "Parents, be the soul support of your children."

★

Quip: Living it up is a quick way to build a reputation that you may be long in living down.

Quote: "If you must choose, take a good name rather than great riches; for to be held in loving esteem is better than silver or gold" (Proverbs 22:1).

Quest: A boy reaching 13 years of age was asked how it felt to be a teenager. "Okay," he answered, "except for the reputation."

Quip: Some people use religion like a
                 bus—they ride on it only when it's going
                 their way.

Quote: "That night the Christians hurried Paul
                 and Silas to Beroea, and, as usual, they
                 went to the synagogue to preach. But
                 the people of Beroea were more open
                 minded than those in Thessalonia, and
                 gladly listened to the message. They
                 searched the Scriptures day by day to
                 check up on Paul and Silas' statements
                 to see if they were really so"
                 (Acts 17:10,11).

Quest: Religious experience is meant to be
                 bread for daily use, not cake for special
                 occasions.

★

Quip: Life is what happens while you're
                 making other plans.

Quote: "For whoever finds me finds life
                 and wins approval from the Lord"
                 (Proverbs 8:35).

Quest: The length of your life is less important
                 than its breadth and depth.

Quip: Life is made up of sleeping, eating, working—and interruptions.

Quote: "I have been crucified with Christ: and I myself no longer live, but Christ lives in me. And the real life I now have within this body is a result of my trusting in the Son of God, who loved me and gave himself for me" (Galatians 2:20).

Quest: Many of us need to pray the prayer of the old Scot, who mostly feared decay from the chin up: "Lord, keep me alive while I'm still living."

★

Quip: Speak well of your enemies—you made them.

Quote: "There is a saying, 'Love your friends and hate your enemies.' But I say: Love your enemies! Pray for those who persecute you! In that way you will be acting as true sons of your Father in heaven. For he gives his sunlight to both the devil and the good, and sends rain on the just and on the unjust too" (Matthew 5:43-45).

Quest: The best way to kill your enemies is to make them your friends.

Quip: A hypocrite is a person who pretends to
              be burying the hatchet when she's only
              digging up dirt.

Quote: "When you give a gift to a beggar, don't
              shout about it as the hypocrites
              do—blowing trumpets in the synagogues
              and streets to call attention to their acts
              of charity! I tell you in all earnestness,
              they have received all the reward they
              will ever get" (Matthew 6:2).

Quest: Hypocrisy is a homage that vice pays to
              virtue (La Rochefoucauld).

                                ★

Quip: If you have a disagreeable duty to
              perform at twelve noon, do not spoil
              nine, ten, or eleven and all between with
              the color of twelve.

Quote: "So if you are standing before the altar
              in the Temple, offering a sacrifice to
              God, and suddenly remember that a
              friend has something against you, leave
              your sacrifice there beside the altar and
              go and apologize and be reconciled to
              him, and then come and offer your
              sacrifice to God. Come to terms quickly
              with your enemy before it is too late
              and he drags you into court and you are
              thrown into a debtor's cell, for you will
              stay there until you have paid the last
              penny" (Matthew 5:23-26).

Quest: When you have a number of
              disagreeable duties to perform always
              do the most disagreeable first (Quincy).

Quip: You can't kill time without injuring eternity.

Quote: "Don't store up treasures here on earth where they can erode away or may be stolen. Store them in heaven where they will never lose their value, and are safe from thieves. If your profits are in heaven your heart will be there too" (Matthew 6:19-21).

Quest: Days are like suitcases. By careful arrangement, some people can pack more into them than other people can.

★

Quip: Many people will not read a Bible but will read a Christian.

Quote: "Don't let anyone think little of you because you are young. Be their ideal; let them follow the way you teach and live; be a pattern for them in your love, your faith, and your clean thoughts. Until I get there, read and explain the Scriptures to the church; preach God's Word" (1 Timothy 4:12,13).

Quest: He who shall introduce into public affairs the principles of primitive Christianity will revolutionize the world (Franklin).

Quip: He who rolls up sleeves seldom loses
               shirt.

Quote: "Work hard and become a leader; be
               lazy and never succeed"
               (Proverbs 12:24).

Quest: Christianity is a roll-up-your-sleeves
               opportunity.

★

Quip: If you can't be a Christian where you
               are, you can't be one anywhere.

Quote: "For I can do everything God asks me to
               with the help of Christ who gives me the
               strength and power" (Philippians 4:13).

Quest: I am only one, but I am one; I cannot do
               everything, but I can do something.
               What I can do, I ought to do. And what I
               ought to do, by God's grace, I will do.

Quip: Is your Christianity ancient history or
              current news? (Shoemaker).

Quote: ''I want those already wise to become
              the wiser and become leaders by
              exploring the depths of meaning in
              those nuggets of truth'' (Proverbs 1:5,6).

Quest: Whatever makes men good Christians
              also makes them good citizens
              (Webster).

                          ★

Quip: Guidance means that I can count on
              God; commitment means that God can
              count on me.

Quote: ''Trust the Lord completely; don't ever
              trust yourself. In everything you do, put
              God first, and he will direct you and
              crown your efforts with success''
              (Proverbs 3:5,6).

Quest: The world has yet to see what God can
              do with a man completely dedicated to
              Him (Moody).

Quip: A hopeless pessimist is always building dungeons in the air.

Quote: "In the same way, we can see and understand only a little about God now, as if we were peering at his reflection in a poor mirror; but someday we are going to see him in his completeness, face to face. Now all that I know is hazy and blurred, but then I will see everything clearly, just as clearly as God sees into my heart right now" (1 Corinthians 13:12).

Quest: A pessimist is someone who feels bad when he feels good for fear he'll feel worse when he feels better.

★

Quip: You have to be pretty low for a molehill to look like a mountain.

Quote: "I have told you all this so that you will have peace of heart and mind. Here on earth you will have many trials and sorrows; but cheer up, for I have overcome the world" (John 16:33).

Quest: There is no danger of eyestrain if you look on the bright side of things.

Quip: No pain, no gain!

Quote: "After you have suffered a little while, our God, who is full of kindness through Christ, will give you his eternal glory. He personally will come and pick you up, and set you firmly in place, and make you stronger than ever" (1 Peter 5:10)

Quest: After crosses and losses, men grow humbler and wiser (Franklin).

★

Quip: Success is sweet, but its secret is sweat. Fortunately, no one has ever drowned himself in sweat.

Quote: "He who loves wisdom loves his own best interest and will be a success" (Proverbs 19:8).

Quest: Success humbles the great man, astonishes the common man, and puffs up the little man.

Quip: Thousands of nuts hold a car
               together—but one can scatter it all over
               the road.

Quote: "The man who strays away from
               common sense will end up dead!"
               (Proverbs 21:16).

Quest: The road to ruin is always in good
               repair; the travelers pay the expense of
               it.

                          ★

Quip: There are two periods in a man's life
               when he doesn't understand
               women—before and after marriage.

Quote: "For the value of wisdom is far above
               rubies; nothing can be compared with it.
               Wisdom and good judgment live
               together, for wisdom knows where to
               discover knowledge and understanding"
               (Proverbs 8:11,12).

Quest: Humanity's great need is not for more
               money, but for more understanding.

Quip: Thinking occurs when your mouth stays shut and your head keeps talking to itself.

Quote: "A good man's mind is filled with honest thoughts; an evil man's head is crammed with lies" (Proverbs 12:5).

Quest: Most of our difficulties stem from inconsistent thinking, not lack of thoughts. We wrestle inconclusively with our problems by thinking about them in a random manner.

★

Quip: If you must slander anyone, don't speak it, but write it—write it in the sand near the water's edge.

Quote: "To hate is to be a liar; to slander is to be a fool" (Proverbs 10:18).

Quest: A wise old owl lived in an oak; the more he saw the less he spoke; the less he spoke the more he heard; why can't we all be like that bird?

Quip: The pleasures of sin are for a season,
               but the consequences of sin are forever.

Quote: "It was by faith that Moses, when he
               grew up, refused to be treated as the
               grandson of the king, but chose to share
               ill-treatment with God's people instead
               of enjoying the fleeting pleasures of sin.
               He thought that it was better to
               suffer for the promised Christ than to
               own all the treasures of Egypt, for he
               was looking forward to the great reward
               that God would give him" (Hebrews
               11:24-26).

Quest: Sin we have explained away;
               unfortunately, the sinners stay.

★

Quip: It is better to be silent and be
               considered a fool than to speak and
               remove all doubt.

Quote: "The man of few words and settled mind
               is wise; therefore, even a fool is thought
               to be wise when he is silent. It pays him
               to keep his mouth shut" (Proverbs
               17:27,28).

Quest: I have never been hurt by anything I
               didn't say" (Coolidge).

Quip: Sign on office bulletin board: "In case of fire, don't panic. Simply flee the building with the same reckless abandon that occurs each day at quitting time."

Quote: "Look here, you people who say, 'Today or tomorrow we are going to such and such a town, stay there a year, and open up a profitable business.' How do you know what is going to happen tomorrow.? For the length of your lives is as uncertain as the morning fog—now you see it; soon it is gone" (James 4:13,14).

Quest: Time is a versatile performer. It flies, marches on, heals all wounds, runs out, and will tell (Franklin P. Jones).

★

Quip: The biggest drawback to educational television is that most children want to major in cartoons, cowboys, and Indians.

Quote: "I would have you learn this great fact: that a life of doing right is the wisest life there is. If you live by that kind of life, you'll not limp or stumble as you run. Carry out my instructions; don't forget them, for they will lead you to real living" (Proverbs 4:11-13).

Quest: Children who watch television night and day will go down in history—not to mention mathematics, geography, and grammar.

Quip: The soul would have no rainbows if there were no tears.

Quote: "Those who sow tears shall reap joy. Yes, they go out weeping, carrying seed for sowing, and returning singing, carrying their sheaves" (Psalm 126:5,6).

Quest: It is some relief to weep; grief is satisfied and carried off by tears (Ovid).

★

Quip: Why is there never enough time to do right, but always enough time to do it over?

Quote: "Make the most of your chances to tell others the Good News. Be wise in all your contacts with them" (Colossians 4:5).

Quest: God cares about how you use your time because that time is a gift from Him. It is yours to redeem, commit, waste, or even steal. How are you treating your gift?

Quip: When my father found me on the wrong track, he always provided switching facilities.

Quote: "If you refuse to discipline your son, it proves you don't love him; for if you love him you will be prompt to punish him" (Proverbs 13:24).

Quest: The reason some parents no longer lead their children in the right direction is because they aren't going that way themselves.

★

Quip: No wonder it's tough to be a teenager. Half the grownups tell him to find himself, and the other half tell him to get lost!

Quote: "Every young man who listens to me and obeys my instructions will be given wisdom and good sense. Yes, if you want better insight and discernment, and are searching for them as you would for lost money or hidden treasure, then wisdom will be given you, and knowledge of God himself; you will soon learn the importance of reverence for the Lord and of trusting him" (Proverbs 2:1-5).

Quest: It's foolish to worry about confused teenagers. Give them time and they'll grow up to be confused adults!

Quip: The accent may be on youth, but the
            stress is still on the parents.

Quote: "Listen to your father's advice and don't
            despise an old mother's experience. Get
            the facts at any price, and hold on tightly
            to all the good sense you can get. The
            father of a godly man has cause for
            joy—what pleasure a wise son is! So give
            your parents joy!" (Proverbs 23:22-25).

Quest: Really, the younger generation isn't so
            bad. It's just that they have more critics
            than models.

                            ★

Quip: Poise is the act of raising your eyebrows
            instead of the roof.

Quote: "A wise man controls his temper.
            He knows that anger causes mistakes"
            (Proverbs 14:29).

Quest: Funny thing about temper: You can't get
            rid of it by losing it.

Quip: No matter what happens, there is always someone who knew it would.

Quote: "A wicked man is always in trouble throughout his life. He is surrounded by terrors, and if there are good days they will soon be gone. He dares not go out into the darkness, lest he be murdered. He wanders around begging for food. He lives in fear, distress, and anguish. His enemies conquer him as a king defeats his foes" (Job 15:20-24).

Quest: The most destructive acid in the world is found in a sour disposition.

★

Quip: It isn't hard to make a mountain out of a molehill. Just add a little dirt.

Quote: "Keep your mouth closed and you'll stay out of trouble" (Proverbs 21:23).

Quest: Speak but little and well, if you would be esteemed as a man of merit (Trench).

Quip: Deception is a short blanket—if you pull
                it over your face, you expose your feet.

Quote: "Don't you know that those doing such
                things have no share in the Kingdom of
                God? Don't fool yourselves. Those who
                live immoral lives, who are idol
                worshipers, adulterers or homosex-
                uals—will have no share in his kingdom.
                Neither will thieves or greedy people,
                drunkards, slanderers, or robbers"
                (1 Corinthians 6:9,10).

Quest: You can fool some of the people all of
                the time, and all of the people some of
                the time, but you cannot fool all of the
                people all of the time (Lincoln).

★

Quip: Business will put away encouraging
                profits when it put away discouraging
                prophets.

Quote: "But Moses told the people, 'Don't be
                afraid. Just stand where you are and
                watch, and you will see the wonderful
                way the Lord will rescue you today. The
                Egyptians you are looking at—you will
                never see them again. The Lord will fight
                for you, and you won't need to lift a
                finger!' " (Exodus 14:13,14).

Quest: The man who deals in sunshine is the
                man who gets the crowds; he does a lot
                more business than the man who
                peddles clouds.

Quip: If you don't stand for something, you'll
               fall for everything.

Quote: "So, my dear brothers, since future
               victory is sure, be strong and steady,
               always abounding in the Lord's work, for
               you know that nothing you do for the
               Lord is ever wasted as it would be if
               there were no resurrection"
               (1 Corinthians 15:58).

Quest: The difference between perseverance
               and obstinacy is that one often comes
               from a strong will, and the other from a
               strong won't.

                              ★

Quip: Some students never let studying
               interfere with their education.

Quote: "A wise man is hungry for truth,
               while the mocker feeds on trash"
               (Proverbs 15:14).

Quest: An educational system isn't worth a
               great deal if it teaches children how to
               make a living but doesn't teach them
               how to live.

Quip: Some students drink from the fountain
of knowledge, while others just gargle.

Quote: "Yes, if you want better insight and
discernment, and are searching for them
as you would for lost money or hidden
treasure, then wisdom will be given, and
knowledge of God himself; you will soon
learn the importance of reverence for
the Lord and of trusting him"
(Proverbs 2:3-5).

Quest: You can lead a youth to college but you
can not make him think.

★

Quip: Fashion is something that goes in one
year and out the other.

Quote: "Those in frequent contact with the
exciting things the world offers should
make good use of their opportunities
without stopping to enjoy them; for the
world in its present form will soon be
gone" (1 Corinthians 7:31).

Quest: All change is not growth, as all
movement is not forward.

Quip: Success is relative—the more success the more relatives.

Quote: "He who loves wisdom loves his own best interest and will be a success" (Proverbs 19:8).

Quest: There is a great deal of practical benefit in making a few mistakes early in life.

★

Quip: One, on God's side, is a majority.

Quote: "Dear young friends, you belong to God and have already won your fight with those who are against Christ, because there is someone in your hearts who is stronger than any evil teacher in this wicked world" (1 John 4:4).

Quest: My concern is not whether God is on our side; my great concern is to be on God's side, for God is always right (Lincoln).

Quip: If doubt knocks on your door, send faith
               to answer.

Quote: "If you want to know what God wants
               you to do, ask him, and he will gladly
               tell you, for he is always ready to give a
               bountiful supply of wisdom to all who
               ask him; he will not resent it. But when
               you ask him, be sure that you really ex-
               pect him to tell you, for a doubtful mind
               will be as unsettled as a wave of the sea
               that is driven and tossed by the wind"
               (James 1:5,6).

Quest: Three men were walking on a wall—
               Feeling, Faith, and Fact. Feeling took an
               awful fall, and Faith was taken back.
               Faith was so close to Feeling that he
               then fell down too, but Fact remained
               and pulled Faith up, and Faith brought
               Feeling too.

                              ★

Quip: As the mama whale said to the baby
               whale, "It's only when you're spouting
               that you get harpooned."

Quote: "Keep your mouth closed and you'll stay
               out of trouble" (Proverbs 21:23).

Quest: Be sure your brain is in gear before
               engaging your mouth.

Quip: You can tell when you're on the right road—it's uphill.

Quote: "Work hard and become a leader; be lazy and never succeed" (Proverbs 12:24).

Quest: All the roads to success and achievement are uphill.

★

Quip: Time is so powerful it is given to us only in small doses.

Quote: "Teach us to number our days and recognize how few they are; help us to spend them as we should" (Psalm 90:12).

Quest: No matter how you used yesterday, you received 24 hours today.

Quip: A drinking man commits suicide on the installment plan.

Quote: "Woe to you who get up early in the morning to go on long drinking bouts that last until late at night—woe to you drunken bums" (Isaiah 5:11).

Quest: All excess is ill, but drunkeness is of the worst sort. It spoils health, dismounts the mind, and unmans men. It reveals secrets and is quarrelsome, lascivious, impudent, dangerous, and bad (Jefferson).

★

Quip: Duties are the tasks we anticipate with distaste, perform with reluctance, and brag about forever.

Quote: "Here is my final conclusion: fear God and obey his commandments, for this is the entire duty of man. For God will judge us for everything we do, including every hidden thing, good or bad" (Ecclesiastes 12:13,14).

Quest: Let us have faith that right makes might, and in that faith let us, to the end, dare to do our duty as we understand it (Lincoln).

Quip: He who exceeds the speed limit driving into the next county may wind up in the next world.

Quote: "It is dangerous and sinful to rush into the unknown. A man may ruin his chances by his own foolishness and then blame it on the Lord" (Proverbs 19:2,3).

Quest: It's better to be a few minutes late down here than too early up there.

★

Quip: A rumor is about as hard to unspread as butter.

Quote: "A gossip goes around spreading rumors, while a trustworthy man tries to quiet them" (Proverbs 11:13).

Quest: Unfortunately, rumor goes round the world while truth is putting on its boots.

Index